Oxford Children's Rhyming Words

Written by
John Foster

Illustrated by
Charlotte Canty, Katie Saunders,
Rupert Van Wyk and Melanie Williamson

OXFORD
UNIVERSITY PRESS

My name is

. . . .

OXFORD
UNIVERSITY PRESS

Great Clarendon Street, Oxford, OX2 6DP

Oxford University Press is a department of the University of Oxford.
It furthers the University's objective of excellence in research, scholarship,
and education by publishing worldwide.

Oxford is a registered trade mark of Oxford University Press
in the UK and in certain other countries

Text © John Foster 2004, 2003, 2021

The moral rights of the author have been asserted

This title is adapted from *Oxford Children's Rhyming Dictionary*, 2004
and *Oxford First Rhyming Dictionary*, 2003

First published 2021

Database right Oxford University Press (maker)

British Library Cataloguing in Publication Data available

ISBN: 978-0-19-277804-8

10 9 8 7 6 5 4 3 2 1

Paper used in the production of this book is a natural,
recyclable product made from wood grown in sustainable forests.
The manufacturing process conforms to the environmental regulations
of the country of origin.

Printed in China

Oxford OWL

For school
Discover eBooks, inspirational
resources, advice and support

For home
Helping your child's learning
with free eBooks, essential
tips and fun activities

www.oxfordowl.co.uk

Oxford Corpus

You can trust this book
to be up to date, relevant
and engaging because
it is powered by the
Oxford Corpus, a unique
living database of children's
and adults' language.

Acknowledgements

Illustrations by Charlotte Canty,
Katie Saunders, Melanie Williamson
and Rupert Van Wyk

Contents

How to use this book

Have you ever wanted to write a poem, but you can't think of enough rhyming words? Or perhaps you want to write a song or a rap? It can be hard to find words that rhyme with each other, so this book is here to help you.

Using the key words or the index of rhyming sounds, you'll have lots of rhyming words at your fingertips, so you can get started on writing your song or poem!

Key words

A key word is a word that you use very often. In this dictionary, the key words are in **bold**. You can look up a key word and find a list of other words that rhyme with it.

The alphabet

The key words in this book are listed in alphabetical order. There is an alphabet line down the side of each page to help you to find your way around the book.

Rhyming sound and rhyme family

Each key word has a rhyming sound. The rhyming sound can be found in other words too. This is the rhyme family. The words in the rhyme family all have the same sound at the end so they rhyme with each other. They also have the same spelling pattern.

Example

key word	rhyming sound
air	**-air**

rhyme family

chair despair fair flair hair lair
mid-air pair repair stair unfair

Sometimes there are several words from one rhyme family which rhyme with words from another rhyme family.

Example

-air rhymes with **-are**

aware bare beware blare care compare dare declare
fare glare hare mare nightmare prepare rare scare
share snare software spare square stare

-air rhymes with **-aire**

billionaire millionaire solitaire

And sometimes there are words that rhyme with the key word but have a different spelling pattern.

Example

Other words with different spellings that rhyme with **air**

**bear pear prayer swear their
there they're wear where**

Rhymes

There are lots of rhymes dotted throughout this book. You can use these as a starting point for rhymes of your own.

A jaguar from Zanzibar
Learned to play the bass guitar.
Now he's a famous movie star
And drives round in a racing car.

Tips

Throughout this book there are tips to help you with writing poems and other rhymes. Look out for them as you use the book.

Index

This book has two indexes. The A to Z index on page 129 lists every word in this dictionary. The key words are printed in bold type. This index will tell you the page where you will find the rhyming word you are looking for. The index of rhyming sounds on page 126 lists every rhyming sound in this book. You can look up the sounds that you want to make rhymes with and go straight to the key word.

Activities

There is a 'Write your own poetry' section on page 116. This suggests things you can do to practise making up rhymes and writing rhyming poems.

These are the features of the dictionary:

alphabet   key word   rhyming sound

capital letter

letter

rhyming words

different rhyme families

rhyme

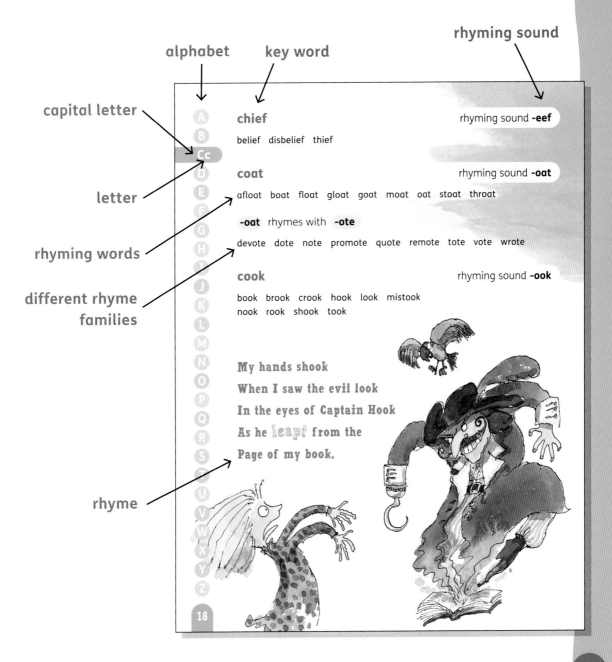

chief   rhyming sound **-eef**

belief disbelief thief

coat   rhyming sound **-oat**

afloat boat float gloat goat moat oat stoat throat

-oat rhymes with **-ote**

devote dote note promote quote remote tote vote wrote

cook   rhyming sound **-ook**

book brook crook hook look mistook
nook rook shook took

My hands shook
When I saw the evil look
In the eyes of Captain Hook
As he leapt from the
Page of my book.

18

Aa

act

rhyming sound **-act**

abstract attract compact contact contract distract exact extract
fact impact interact pact react subtract tact

-act rhymes with **-acked**

backed backpacked backtracked cracked hijacked humpbacked
lacked packed quacked sacked smacked snacked stacked
tracked unpacked whacked

affect

rhyming sound **-ect**

effect incorrect perfect

air

rhyming sound **-air**

chair despair fair flair hair lair mid-air pair repair stair unfair

-air rhymes with **-are**

aware bare beware blare care compare dare declare fare
glare hare mare nightmare prepare rare scare share snare
software spare square stare

-air also rhymes
with **-aire**

billionaire millionaire
solitaire

Other words with different spellings
that rhyme with **air**

**bear pear prayer swear their
there they're wear where**

animal
rhyming sound sounds like **-ul**

actual   capital   hospital   illegal   immortal
medal   national   natural   pedal   special   usual

-ul   rhymes with   **-le**

apple   bicycle   bottle   circle   illegible
impossible   little   meddle
people   possible

-ul   also rhymes with   **-el**

camel   squirrel   tinsel   travel   tunnel

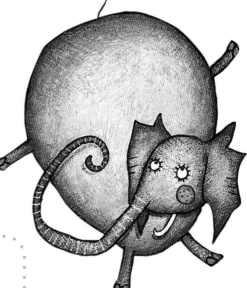

Other words with different spellings
that rhyme with **animal**

fossil   nostril   pencil

ant
rhyming sound **-ant**

currant   descendant   elegant   elephant   pant   rant   scant

arm
rhyming sound **-arm**

alarm   charm   farm   harm

-arm   rhymes with   **-alm**

calm   palm

ask
rhyming sound **-ask**

bask   cask   flask   mask   task

Bb

bang

rhyming sound **-ang**

boomerang clang fang gang hang overhang pang
rang sang slang sprang tang twang

bank

rhyming sound **-ank**

blank clank crank dank drank frank lank plank
prank rank sank shrank stank tank thank yank

beach

rhyming sound **-each**

bleach each peach preach reach teach

-each rhymes with **-eech**

beech screech speech

My sister gave a **screech**
as she bit through the slug in her peach.

belt
rhyming sound **-elt**

dwelt   felt   knelt   melt   pelt   spelt   welt

> Another word with a different spelling that rhymes with **belt**
>
> **dealt**

big
rhyming sound **-ig**

dig   earwig   fig   gig   jig   oil rig   pig   rig
sprig   swig   twig   whirligig   wig

bike
rhyming sound **-ike**

alike   dislike   hike   like   pike   spike   strike
trike

bird
rhyming sound **-ird**

ladybird   third

> Other words with different spellings that rhyme with **bird**
>
> **absurd   blurred   heard   herd   nerd   preferred
> purred   stirred   whirred   word**

black
rhyming sound **-ack**

attack back backpack bareback crack flapjack hack
haystack horseback jack knack lack lumberjack pack
piggyback quack rack rucksack sack shack slack smack
snack soundtrack stack tack track unpack whack

Other words with different spellings that
rhyme with **black**

**anorak kayak mac maniac
plaque tarmac yak**

bone
rhyming sound **-one**

alone clone cone drone lone megaphone ozone phone
postpone prone stone throne time zone tombstone
tone trombone xylophone zone

-one rhymes with **-own**

blown flown grown known own shown sown thrown

Other words with different spellings that
rhyme with **bone**

groan loan moan sewn

boot

rhyming sound **-oot**

beetroot   hoot   loot   reboot   root   scoot   shoot   toot

-oot rhymes with **-ute**

acute   brute   chute   cute   dilute   dispute   execute   flute
minute   mute   parachute   pollute   salute   substitute

Other words with different spellings that
rhyme with **boot**

fruit   newt   suit

An elephant in a parachute,

A koala bear playing the flute,

A penguin whizzing down a chute,

And a hippopotamus in a suit.

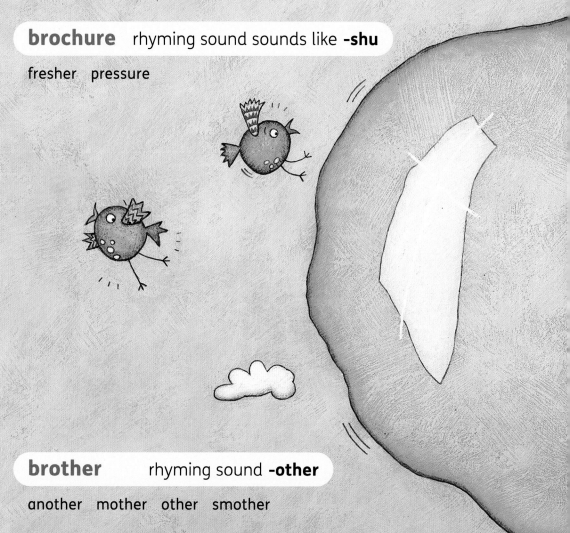

A
Bb
C
D
E
F
G
H
I
J
K
L
M
N
O
P
Q
R
S
T
U
V
W
X
Y
Z

boss   rhyming sound **-oss**

across albatross candyfloss cross floss
gloss loss moss toss

bounce   rhyming sound **-ounce**

announce flounce ounce pounce
pronounce trounce

bridge   rhyming sound **-idge**

fridge midge porridge ridge

brochure   rhyming sound sounds like **-shu**

fresher pressure

brother   rhyming sound **-other**

another mother other smother

bubble   rhyming sound **-ubble**

rubble   stubble

-ubble also rhymes with **-ouble**

double   trouble

Oh dear! I'm in trouble.
I shouldn't have blown
that bubblegum bubble!

Cc

car rhyming sound **-ar**

afar ajar bar caviar cigar far guitar jaguar jar
scar spar star superstar tar tsar

Other words with different
spellings that rhyme with **car**

**aha are baa bizarre ha
ha-ha ma pa**

A jaguar from Zanzibar
Learned to play the bass guitar.
Now he's a famous movie star
And drives round in a racing car!

cart   rhyming sound **-art**

apart art chart dart depart part smart start tart

Another word with a different spelling that rhymes with **cart**

heart

catch   rhyming sound **-atch**

batch hatch latch match mismatch patch scratch snatch thatch

-atch rhymes with **-ach**

attach detach

Think about what you want your rhyme to be. Should it be silly and funny or do you want it to tell a story? Look at page 116 onwards for some ideas.

cave   rhyming sound **-ave**

behave brave crave forgave gave grave heatwave knave microwave pave rave save shave shockwave wave

a b **Cc** d e f g h i j k l m n o p q r s t u v w x y z

chief

rhyming sound **-eef**

belief   disbelief   thief

coat

rhyming sound **-oat**

afloat   boat   float   gloat   goat   moat   oat   stoat   throat

-oat rhymes with **-ote**

devote   dote   note   promote   quote   remote   tote
vote   wrote

cook

rhyming sound **-ook**

book   brook   crook   hook   look   mistook
nook   rook   shook   took

My hands shook
When I saw the evil look
In the eyes of Captain Hook
As he leapt from the
Page of my book.

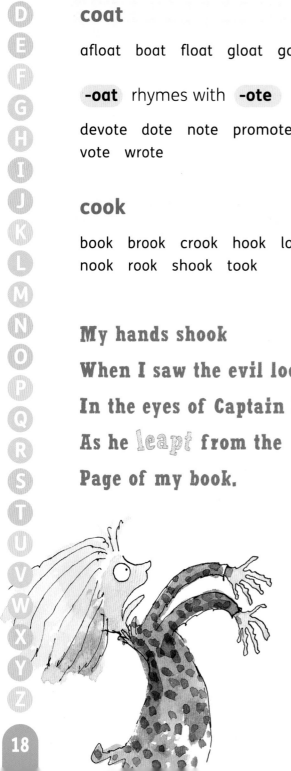

At dawn I saw a unicorn.
I watched it grazing on the lawn,
The sunlight glinting on its horn.

corn

rhyming sound **-orn**

acorn adorn born forlorn horn morn scorn shorn
sworn thorn torn unicorn worn

-orn rhymes with **-awn**

dawn drawn fawn frogspawn lawn pawn sawn yawn

Other words with different spellings that rhyme with **corn**
airborne borne leprechaun

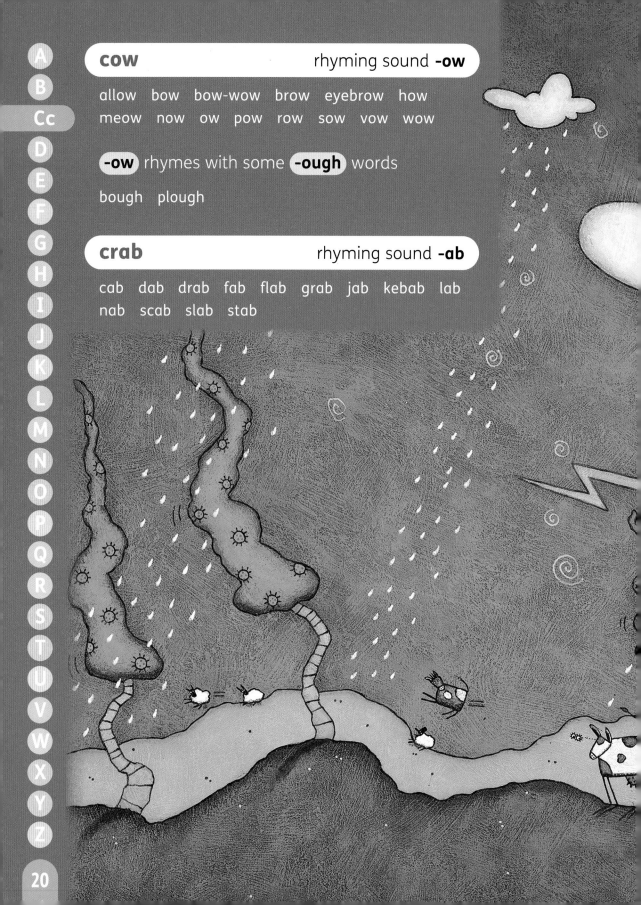

cow
rhyming sound **-ow**

allow   bow   bow-wow   brow   eyebrow   how
meow   now   ow   pow   row   sow   vow   wow

-ow rhymes with some **-ough** words

bough   plough

crab
rhyming sound **-ab**

cab   dab   drab   fab   flab   grab   jab   kebab   lab
nab   scab   slab   stab

A
B
Cc
D
E
F
G
H
I
J
K
L
M
N
O
P
Q
R
S
T
U
V
W
X
Y
Z

crash — rhyming sound **-ash**

ash bash cash clash dash flash gash
gnash hash lash mash rash sash slapdash
slash smash splash thrash trash whiplash

Lightning flash
Thunder crash
Winds lash
Trees thrash
Raindrops splash
Storms smash!

crept — rhyming sound **-ept**

accept adept except inept intercept
kept slept swept wept

> Other words with different spellings
> that rhyme with **crept**
>
> leapt stepped

Dd

dad   rhyming sound **-ad**

bad   clad   fad   glad   had   lad   mad   nomad   pad   sad

> Another word with a different spelling that rhymes with **dad**
>
> **add**

**"You're a good lad," said Dad.
"But your music drives me mad!"**

dance   rhyming sound **-ance**

advance   chance   entrance   France   glance   lance
prance   stance   trance

dark

rhyming sound **-ark**

aardvark ark bark embark hark landmark lark mark park remark shark spark

"My bite is worse than my **bark**," said the **shark**. "With my teeth I leave my **mark**!"

dinner
rhyming sound **-inner**

beginner   inner   sinner   spinner   thinner
winner

dog
rhyming sound **-og**

agog   bog   clog   cog   flog   fog   frog   grog
hog   jog   log   slog

-og also rhymes with some **-ogue** words

catalogue   monologue

I know a dog who thinks he's a frog.
I know a frog who thinks he's a dog.
Who is who?
Is the dog a frog or the frog a dog?

dream
rhyming sound **-eam**

beam   cream   daydream   gleam   ice cream
scream   seam   steam   stream   team

-eam also rhymes with **-eem**

redeem   seem   teem

Other words with different
spellings that rhyme with **dream**

**extreme   scheme   supreme
theme**

Why not try
thinking about one set
of rhyming sounds like this:

I was sitting by a **stream**.
When I dropped my
ice cream.
And I gave a loud **scream**.
But it was only a **dream**.

dress
rhyming sound **-ess**

address bless business chess confess cress depress
distress excess express guess happiness helpless
hopeless impress kindness less loneliness mess
oppress penniless plainness possess press princess
progress sadness stress success unless

> Another word with a different spelling
> that rhymes with **dress**
>
> **yes**

duck
rhyming sound **-uck**

buck chuck cluck luck muck pluck struck stuck
suck truck tuck yuck

dust
rhyming sound **-ust**

adjust bust crust disgust gust just must rust
thrust trust

Ee

ear rhyming sound **-ear**

appear clear dear disappear fear gear
hear near reappear rear shear smear
spear tear year

-ear rhymes with **-eer**

beer buccaneer career cheer
deer engineer jeer leer
mountaineer musketeer peer
pioneer sheer sneer steer
veer volunteer

-ear also rhymes with **-ere**

atmosphere here mere persevere
revere severe sincere sphere

We all gave a cheer
as the wizard made our teacher
disappear.

Other words with different spellings
that rhyme with **ear**

**cashier cavalier frontier
gondolier pier souvenir weir**

east
rhyming sound **-east**

beast   feast   least   yeast

-east rhymes with **-eased**

ceased   creased   deceased   greased
increased   released

elf
rhyming sound **-elf**

bookshelf   herself   himself   itself   myself
self   shelf   yourself

end
rhyming sound **-end**

ascend   attend   bend   blend   defend
depend   descend   extend   friend   intend
lend   mend   offend   pretend   recommend
send   spend   suspend   tend   trend

ever
rhyming sound **-ever**

clever   forever   however   never   sever
whatever   whenever   wherever   whichever
whoever

Ff

face rhyming sound **-ace**

ace brace commonplace disgrace embrace fireplace grace
lace misplace pace place race replace shoelace space trace

-ace rhymes with **-ase**

base bookcase case chase database staircase suitcase

I took my place beside Grace
At the start of the three-legged race
But my lace came undone
When we started to run
And Grace fell flat on her face!

family

rhyming sound **-ly**

angrily badly completely early gently humbly nobly only
probably sadly simply

-ly rhymes with **-lly**

accidentally actually basically comically dramatically finally
frantically occasionally usually

find

rhyming sound **-ind**

behind bind blind grind kind mind remind rewind rind
unkind wind

-ind rhymes with **-ined**

dined fined lined mined
pined whined

> Another word with a different spelling that rhymes with **find**
>
> **signed**

fire

rhyming sound **-ire**

admire bonfire desire dire empire hire inquire inspire quagmire
spire squire tire umpire vampire wire

> Other words with different spellings that rhyme with **fire**
>
> **choir flyer friar fryer higher
> liar tyre**

first rhyming sound **-irst**

thirst

> Other words with different spellings that rhyme with **first**
>
> **burst cursed nursed
> rehearsed worst**

fish
rhyming sound **-ish**

dish perish punish rubbish selfish squish
swish vanish wish

Other words with different spellings that rhyme with **fish**

liquorice

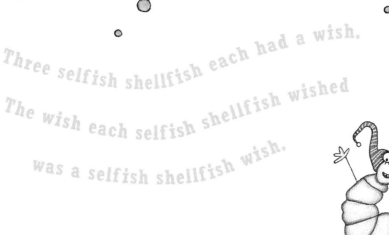

Three selfish shellfish each had a wish.

The wish each selfish shellfish wished

was a selfish shellfish wish.

five
rhyming sound **-ive**

alive arrive dive drive hive jive live revive
strive survive

Another word with a different spelling that rhymes with **five**

I've

flag
rhyming sound **-ag**

bag brag crag drag gag hag lag nag rag sag snag
stag swag tag wag zigzag

food

brood   mood

-ood rhymes with **-ewed**

brewed   chewed   mewed   screwed   slewed   viewed

-ood also rhymes with **-ooed**

booed   boo-hooed   cooed   mooed   shampooed
shooed   tattooed   wooed

-ood also rhymes with **-ude**

altitude   attitude   crude   exclude   gratitude
include   intrude   nude   rude   solitude

-ood also rhymes with **-ued**

argued   barbecued   glued
pursued   rescued   sued

fox

rhyming sound **-ox**

box   cox   ox   pox

-ox rhymes with **-ocks**

blocks   clocks   docks   flocks   frocks   knocks   locks
mocks   rocks   shocks   socks   stocks

Oh Goldilocks! Goldilocks!
I simply cannot deny
The wafting scent of your old socks
Is enough to make me cry!

freeze

rhyming sound **-eeze**

breeze sneeze squeeze wheeze

-eeze rhymes with **-ees**

agrees bees chimpanzees
degrees dungarees fees flees
frees knees referees sees
toffees trees

-eeze rhymes with **-ease**

disease ease please tease

Chimpanzees in dungarees

Swing with ease on the trapeze,

While bees on skis

Struggle to juggle packs of peas.

Other words with different spellings that rhyme with **freeze**

babies carries
cheese chimneys
copies donkeys fleas
keys monkeys peas
seas seize skis teas
these trapeze

fur

rhyming sound **-ur**

blur   occur   slur   spur

-ur rhymes with **-ir**

fir   sir   stir

-ur also rhymes with **-er**

after   answer   badger   better   buzzer   character
consider   father   fatter   gardener   grander   her   hunter
jumper   nicer   otter   prefer   quarter   quicker   remember
runner   sadder   sister   slipper   summer   tiger   wander
water   weather   winter

-ur also rhymes with some **-ar** words

calendar   Caspar   grammar   irregular
particular   popular   regular   sugar

Other words with
different spellings
that rhyme with **fur**

author   copier
centre   happier
neighbour
peculiar   purr
were   whirr

Always call a tiger "Sir"

And do not try to stroke his fur

For tigers are well known to grrr!

Gg

gate rhyming sound **-ate**

appreciate ate calculate celebrate concentrate confiscate
crate create date debate decorate educate estate estimate
exaggerate fascinate fate frustrate grate hate investigate
irritate Kate late mate operate plate rate redecorate separate
skate slate state

-ate rhymes with **-ait**

bait wait

> Other words with
> different spellings that
> rhyme with **gate**
> **eight fete great
> straight weight**

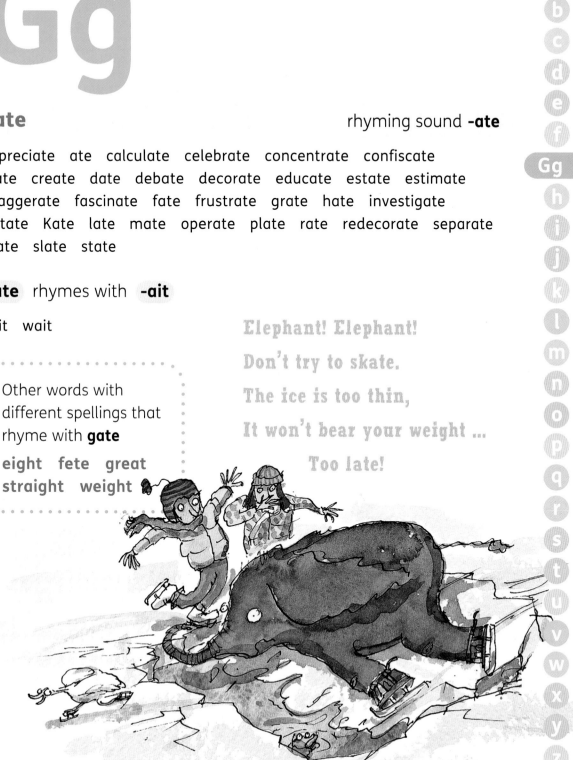

Elephant! Elephant!
Don't try to skate.
The ice is too thin,
It won't bear your weight ...
Too late!

girl

rhyming sound **-irl**

swirl   twirl   whirl

-irl rhymes with **-url**

curl   furl   hurl   unfurl

Other words with different spellings that rhyme with **girl**

earl   pearl

glass

rhyming sound **-ass**

brass   bypass   class   grass   pass   trespass

grape

rhyming sound **-ape**

agape   ape   cape   drape
escape   gape   landscape   scrape
shape   tape

grub

club   cub   dub   hub   hubbub   pub   rub   scrub   shrub
snub   stub   tub

A grubby grub sat in a tub
And sang as he had a good scrub:
"I'm a scrub-a-grub, rub-a-dub grub!"

Hh

hairy   rhyming sound **-airy**

airy   dairy   fairy

-airy rhymes with **-ary**

canary   contrary   Mary   scary   vary   wary

hand   rhyming sound **-and**

and   band   brand   expand   gland   grand   land   sand
stand   strand   understand

-and rhymes with **-anned**

banned   canned   fanned   manned   planned   scanned
spanned   tanned

hat

rhyming sound **-at**

acrobat aristocrat at bat brat cat chat combat fat
flat gnat habitat mat pat pit-a-pat rat rat-a-tat-tat
sat spat splat that vat wombat

There was a young fellow called Matt

Who wanted to look like a cat

His feet were like paws

With retractable claws

And whiskers grew out of his hat.

hen

rhyming sound **-en**

amen Ben den fen glen Ken Len
men pen ten then when wren yen

Another word with a different spelling that rhymes with **hen**

again

hit

rhyming sound **-it**

admit bandit biscuit bit circuit culprit exit fit flit grit habit
it kit knit lit nit omit orbit outfit permit pit quit rabbit sit
split summit twit visit wit

Other words with different spellings that rhyme with **hit**

favourite   opposite

hole — rhyming sound **-ole**

casserole   console   dole   mole   pole   role
sole   stole   tadpole   vole   whole

-ole rhymes with **-oal**

coal   foal   goal   shoal

-ole also rhymes with some **-oll** words

poll   roll   scroll   stroll   troll

Old King Cole scored a very fine goal
A very fine goal scored he,
"Goodness," said Cole,
"I think I'm on a roll"
And his team won 24-3!

40

honey

rhyming sound **-oney**

money

-oney rhymes with **-unny**

bunny   funny   runny   sunny

I eat my peas with honey.
I've done it all my life.
It makes the peas taste funny.
But it keeps them on the knife.

Hh

hood

rhyming sound **-ood**

childhood   deadwood   driftwood   falsehood   good
neighbourhood   stood   understood   wood

-ood rhymes with some **-ould** words

could   should   would

hoop

rhyming sound **-oop**

coop   droop   loop   nincompoop
scoop   sloop   snoop   stoop
swoop   troop   whoop

-oop rhymes with **-oup**

group   soup

house

rhyming sound **-ouse**

louse   mouse   spouse

A mouse and his spouse doing cartwheels round the house.

hunt

rhyming sound **-unt**

blunt   grunt   punt   runt   shunt   stunt

Another word with a different spelling that rhymes with **hunt**

front

hut

rhyming sound **-ut**

but   chestnut   cut   doughnut   glut   gut   jut   nut   rut
shut   strut   tut-tut

Another word with a different spelling that rhymes with **hut**

putt

Ii

ice   rhyming sound **-ice**

advice   dice   lice   mice   nice   price   rice   sacrifice   slice
spice   splice   trice   twice   vice

> Other words with different spellings that rhyme with **ice**
>
> **paradise   precise**

The three blind mice said,

"It's not very nice

Of the farmer's wife

To want to slice

Off our tails with her carving knife!"

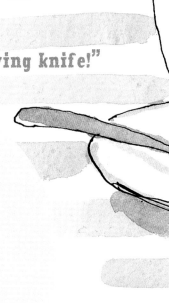

What about
writing a riddle
which needs to be solved?
Can you guess what this word
might be?

My first letter is in **magic**
but not in **sunny**

My second letter is in **twice**
but not in **funny**

My third letter is in **cheese**
but not in **fairy**

My fourth letter is in **three**
but not in **hairy!**

ill

bill brill chill drill fill frill gill grill hill Jill kill
mill pill quill shrill sill skill spill still swill thrill
till will windmill

-ill rhymes with **-il**

daffodil fossil fulfil nil nostril
pencil Phil tranquil until

There once was a boy called Bill
Who sat on a porcupine's quill.
He jumped in the air
'Cause his bottom was bare
And that's why he cannot sit still.

imp

rhyming sound **-imp**

chimp   crimp   limp   primp   scrimp   shrimp   skimp   wimp

improve

rhyming sound sounds like **-oove**

move   prove

ink

rhyming sound **-ink**

blink   brink   chink   clink   drink   kink   link   mink   pink
rink   shrink   sink   slink   stink   think   wink

Another word with a different
spelling that rhymes with **ink**

zinc

itch

rhyming sound **-itch**

ditch   glitch   hitch   pitch   snitch
stitch   switch   twitch   witch

-itch rhymes with **-ich**

ostrich   rich   which

*There were twin witches, Mitch and Titch.
No one could tell which witch was which.*

Jj

jam

rhyming sound **-am**

am cram dam exam gram ham Pam pram program ram Sam scam scram sham slam swam tram wham wigwam yam

> Another word with a different spelling that rhymes with **jam**
>
> **lamb**

jet

rhyming sound **-et**

alphabet basket bet bracelet bucket carpet clarinet cricket duet fidget forget fret gadget get helmet internet jacket let magnet met net pet pocket puppet regret rocket secret set sunset supermarket ticket trumpet upset vet wet yet

-et rhymes with some **-eat** words

sweat threat

-et also rhymes with **-ette**

baguette cassette courgette launderette omelette serviette

> Another word with a different spelling that rhymes with **jet**
>
> **debt**

job
rhyming sound **-ob**

blob bob cob gob hob hobnob knob lob mob rob
snob sob throb

jug
rhyming sound **-ug**

bug chug drug dug glug hug humbug lug mug
plug rug shrug slug smug snug thug tug

A **slimy slug** drank from a **jug**.

A **grubby bug** drank from a **mug**.

Then the **slug** gave the **bug** a **hug!**

jump
rhyming sound **-ump**

bump clump dump frump goosebump hump lump
plump pump rump slump stump thump trump

Kk

keep

rhyming sound **-eep**

asleep beep bleep cheep creep deep jeep peep
seep sheep sleep steep sweep weep

-eep rhymes with **-eap**

cheap heap leap reap

king   rhyming sound **-ing**

beginning boring bring
buzzing ceiling cling
copying crying ding
dropping fling forgetting
gardening hiking humming
hunting jumping
limiting morning
nothing patting
ping replying
ring sing sling
spring sting string
subheading swing thing
wing wring zing

When the bee gave the king a sting
The king did a highland fling.
So his arm ended up in a sling.

kiss

rhyming sound **-iss**

amiss   bliss   dismiss   hiss   miss

Other words with different spellings that rhyme with **kiss**

office   **practice**   **promise**   **service**   **this**

I'll be good, Mum, just promise me this:
You won't try to give me a kiss
In the playground. Just give it a miss!

knock

rhyming sound **-ock**

lock   clock   crock   dock   flock   frock   lock   mock   rock   shock
ock   stock   tick-tock

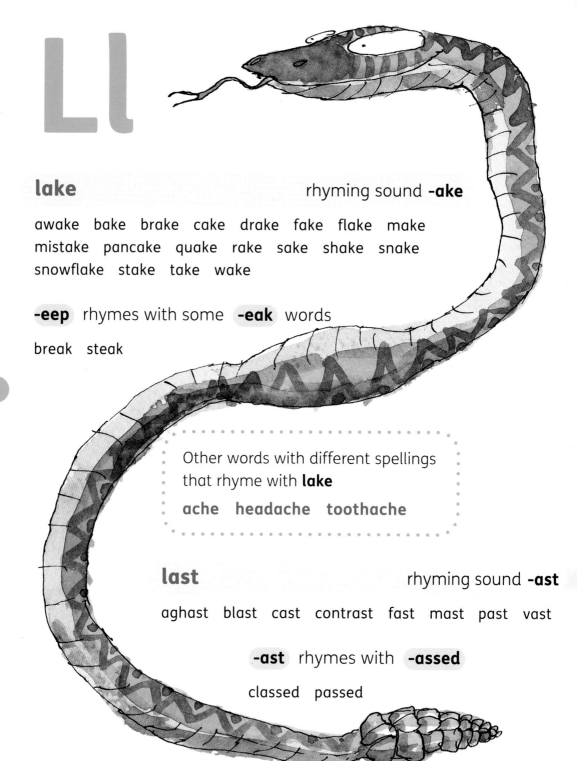

Ll

lake   rhyming sound **-ake**

awake bake brake cake drake fake flake make
mistake pancake quake rake sake shake snake
snowflake stake take wake

-eep rhymes with some **-eak** words

break steak

> Other words with different spellings
> that rhyme with **lake**
>
> ache headache toothache

last   rhyming sound **-ast**

aghast blast cast contrast fast mast past vast

-ast rhymes with **-assed**

classed passed

"You'd better run fast," said the pirate to Frank.
"The last past the mast will walk the plank!"

leg rhyming sound **-eg**

beg dreg Greg keg Meg
nutmeg peg

Another word with a different spelling that rhymes with **leg**

egg

lid rhyming sound **-id**

bid did forbid grid hid kid liquid pyramid quid
rapid rid rigid skid slid squid stupid timid undid

I slid back the volt
and undid the locks

To see what lay
hidden in the secret
box.

light

rhyming sound **-ight**

bright   delight   fight   flight   fright   knight   midnight
might   night   outright   playwright   plight   right   sight
slight   stagefright   tight   tonight   twilight   upright   uptight

-ight   rhymes with   **-ite**

appetite   bite   dynamite   excite   ignite   invite   kite   mite
polite   quite   recite   site   spite   sprite   unite   website
white   write

Other words with
different spellings
that rhyme with
light

byte   height

When Dwight Wright had stagefright,
Mrs Wright said, "Don't get uptight, Dwight,
It'll be all right on the night."

After the first night, Dwight Wright
Said, "It went all right.
You were quite right, Mrs Wright."

lord

rhyming sound **-ord**

afford   chord   cord   ford   record   sword

-ord rhymes with **-oard**

aboard   board   cardboard   hoard   keyboard   scoreboard
skateboard

-ord also rhymes with **-ored**

adored   bored   explored   ignored   scored   snored   stored

Other words with different spellings that rhyme with **lord**
**abroard   applaud   award   broad   horde   poured
reward   roared   soared   sword   toward   ward**

love

rhyming sound **-ove**

above   dove   glove   shove

lunch

rhyming sound **-unch**

brunch   bunch   crunch   hunch   munch   punch   scrunch

lung

rhyming sound **-ung**

bung   clung   dung   flung   hung   rung   slung   sprung
strung   stung   sung   swung   wrung

Other words with different spellings that rhyme with **lung**
among   tongue   young

Mm

map   rhyming sound **-ap**

bap cap chap clap flap gap kidnap lap nap overlap rap
sap scrap slap snap strap tap trap unwrap wrap yap zap

On the Clip Clop Clap
All the Flops flip flap
And the Bongles boogle in the breeze.
The Sniggers snip snap

The Trotters trip trap
And the Somersaults sniff and sneeze
The Somersaults sniff and sneeze.

meat   rhyming sound **-eat**

beat bleat cheat defeat eat feat heat neat peat
pleat repeat retreat seat treat wheat

-eat rhymes with **-eet**

discreet feet fleet greet meet parakeet sheet sleet
street sweet

-eat also rhymes with some **-ete** words

athlete compete complete concrete delete

Pete dressed up in a sheet
And went round the street
Knocking on doors
Saying, "Trick or treat?"

But at number thirty four
Pete got more
Than he bargained for,
When a troll opened the door!

So Pete beat a hasty retreat.

merry
rhyming sound **-erry**

berry   cherry   ferry   Terry

Other words with different spellings
that rhyme with **merry**

bury   very

middle
rhyming sound **-iddle**

diddle   fiddle   griddle   riddle   twiddle

mist
rhyming sound **-ist**

chemist   cyclist   fist   insist   list   resist   tourist
twist   wrist

-ist rhymes with **-issed**

dismissed   hissed   kissed   missed

mix
rhyming sound **-ix**

fix   matrix   phoenix   six

-ix rhymes with **-icks**

bricks   broomsticks   chicks   clicks   flicks   gimmicks
kicks   licks   matchsticks   nicks   picks   pricks   sticks
ticks   tricks

moon

afternoon baboon balloon bassoon cartoon croon
harpoon honeymoon lagoon macaroon maroon
noon platoon raccoon saloon soon spoon swoon
tycoon typhoon

A baboon flew
up to the moon.

"Go away!" said the
Man in the Moon

And he burst
the baboon's
balloon.

-oon rhymes with **-une**

dune fortune June Neptune
prune tune

> Another word with a different
> spelling that rhymes with **moon**
>
> **strewn**

Mm

mud

rhyming sound **-ud**

bud cud dud scud spud stud sud thud

Other words with different spellings that rhyme with **mud**

blood flood

mum

rhyming sound **-um**

chum drum glum gum hum plum rum scrum
scum slum strum sum swum tum yum yum-yum

-um rhymes with **-umb**

crumb dumb numb plumb succumb thumb

Other words with different spellings that rhyme with **mum**

**become come
some**

Try a counting rhyme:

One little koala playing on a drum.
Missed a beat when he struck his thumb.

Two little koalas got stuck in the mud
Playing on a river bank after a flood.

Can you think of another verse?

musician

rhyming sound **-cian**

electrician   magician   mathematician   politician

-cian rhymes with **-tion**

action   admiration   completion   fiction   hesitation
information   injection   invention   limitation   mention
motion   position   preparation   section   sensation   station

-cian also rhymes with **-sion** and **-ssion**

admission   collision   comprehension
confession   confusion   decision   discussion
division   expansion   expression   extension
invasion   occasion   permission
possession   tension

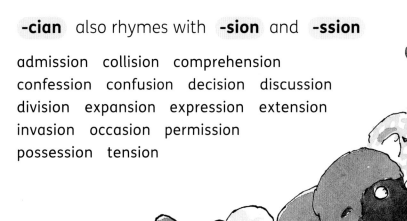

Nn

name rhyming sound **-ame**

became blame came fame flame frame
game lame same shame tame

-ame rhymes with **-aim**

acclaim aim claim exclaim maim

I am the wizard's dragon,
I speak with tongues of flame.
I am the wizard's dragon,
Firesnorter is my name.

neck
rhyming sound **-eck**

beck   check   deck   fleck   peck   speck   wreck

Other words with different spellings that rhyme with **neck**

cheque   Czech   discoteque   high-tech   trek

"Just let me check," said the vampire.
"I think there's a speck
Of blood on your neck."

nettle
rhyming sound **-ettle**

fettle   kettle   settle

-ettle rhymes with **-etal**

metal   petal

nine

rhyming sound **-ine**

airline   brine   combine   define   dine   divine   fine   line
mine   pine   recline   shine   shrine   spine   swine   twine
valentine   vine   whine   wine

-ine   rhymes with   **-ign**

design   resign   sign

It sent a shiver down my spine
When I received a valentine,
Saying, "I think you are divine"
'Cause it was signed 'Frankenstein'!

chose   close   expose   hose   pose   propose   prose   rose   suppose   thos‹

-ose rhymes with **-ows**

arrows   bellows   blows   bows   bungalows   crows   elbows
flows   glows   grows   knows   meadows   mows   rows   shadows
shows   slows   snows   sows   stows   throws   tows

-ose also rhymes with **-oes**

dominoes   foes   goes   hoes   oboes   potatoes   tiptoes   toes
volcanoes   woes

-ose also rhymes with some **-os** words

radios   stereos   videos

When the winter wind blows
An icicle grows on the scarecrow's nose
And it looks just like Pinnochio's!

> Other words
> with different
> spellings that
> rhyme with **nose**
>
> **bulldoze   doze**
> **froze   sews**
> **UFOs**

68

Oo

oak   rhyming sound **-oak**

cloak   croak   soak

-oak rhymes with **-oke**

awoke   bloke   broke   choke
coke   joke   poke   provoke   smoke
spoke   stroke   woke   yoke

> Other words with
> different spellings that
> rhyme with **oak**
>
> **folk   yolk**

oil   rhyming sound **-oil**

boil   broil   coil   foil   recoil   soil
spoil   toil   turmoil

-oil rhymes with **-oyal**

loyal   royal

> Another word with a different
> spelling that rhymes with **oil**
>
> **gargoyle**

old   rhyming sound **-old**

behold   bold   cold   fold
gold   hold   marigold
scaffold   scold   sold   told

Other words with different
spellings that rhyme with **old**

**bowled   cajoled   consoled
controlled   mould   patrolled
polled   rolled   soled   strolled**

"Behold!" said the wizard
And he conjured a room full of gold.
But my blood ran cold,
When he warned,
"My secrets must never
be told."

out

about   blackout   bout   clout   dugout   hideout   knockout   lookout
lout   pout   rout   scout   shootout   shout   snout   spout   stout
throughout   trout   without

> Other words with different spellings that rhyme with **out**
>
> **doubt   drought**

owl

rhyming sound **-owl**

fowl   growl   howl   prowl   scowl   yowl

-owl rhymes with **-owel**

bowel   towel   trowel   vowel

> Another word with a different spelling that rhymes with **owl**
>
> **foul**

Try a rhyming couplet:

I went for a walk and
I saw an owl,

but it looked me in
the eye and it gave
a scowl!

Oo

71

Pp

page   rhyming sound **-age**

age cage engage enrage outrage rage
rampage sage stage teenage upstage wage

"It's like being on stage.

Let me out or pay me a wage!"

The monkey screeched in a rage

As it rattled the bars of its cage.

paint

rhyming sound **-aint**

complaint   faint   quaint   saint   taint

paste

rhyming sound **-aste**

haste   taste   waste

-aste rhymes with **-aced**

braced   disgraced   embraced   faced   graced   laced
paced   placed   raced   replaced   spaced   traced

Another word with a different spelling that rhymes with **paste**

chased   waist

pond

rhyming sound **-ond**

beyond   blond   bond   fond   respond

Another word with a different spelling that rhymes with **pond**

wand

Said the frog in the pond,

"Please kiss me or
wave your wand."

But the princess
didn't respond.

pool

rhyming sound **-ool**

cool   drool   fool   school   spool   stool   toadstool   tool   whirlpool

-ool rhymes with **-ule**

capsule   globule   miniscule
molecule   mule   ridicule
rule   schedule   yule

A mule playing the fool in the pool.

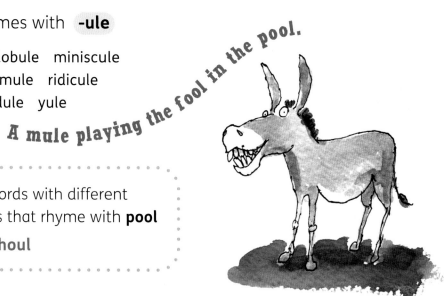

Other words with different
spellings that rhyme with **pool**

fuel   ghoul

post

rhyming sound **-ost**

almost   ghost   host   most   signpost   utmost

-ost rhymes with **-oast**

boast   coast   roast   toast

At the Halloween Ball
Our host was a ghost
Who walked through the wall.

pot

rhyming sound **-ot**

apricot blot cannot clot cot dot earshot forgot got hot
jackpot jot knot lot mascot not plot robot rot Scot shot
slot snot spot swot tot trot

Other words with different spellings that rhyme with **pot**

squat swat what yacht

Old Ned Nott was shot

And Lancelot Shott was not.

So it's better to be Shott than Nott.

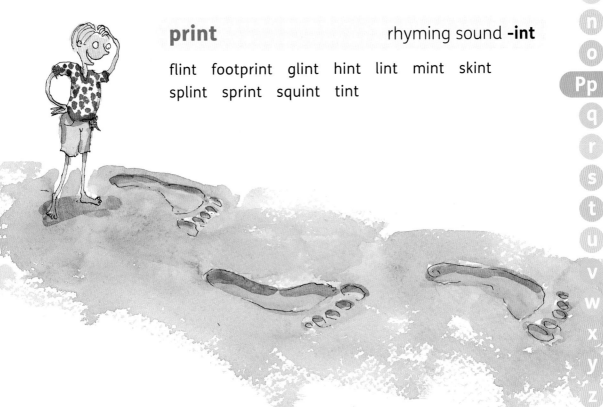

print

rhyming sound **-int**

flint footprint glint hint lint mint skint
splint sprint squint tint

A B C D E F G H I J K L M N O Pp Q R S T U V W X Y Z

puff
rhyming sound **-uff**

bluff buff cuff dandruff duff fluff gruff handcuff
huff scruff scuff snuff stuff

-uff rhymes with some **-ough** words

enough rough tough

pull
rhyming sound **-ull**

bull full

-ull rhymes with **-ul**

armful awful beautiful careful cheerful doubtful
dreadful faithful fearful graceful harmful hopeful
joyful playful plentiful useful wonderful

Another word with a different spelling that rhymes with **pull**

wool

Qq

queen

rhyming sound **-een**

been between canteen green keen preen screen
seen sheen spleen teen thirteen fourteen (etc)

-een rhymes with **-ean**

bean clean glean Jean lean mean wean

-een also rhymes with some **-ine** words

limousine machine magazine routine
sardine submarine tangerine trampoline

-een also rhymes with **-ene**

gene hygiene
scene serene

"I'm a queen," said Kathleen.
"We've been filming a scene.
That's my picture in a magazine
And over there's my limousine."
"Dream on," said Shaheen.

quick

rhyming sound **-ick**

brick chick click flick gimmick kick lick limerick pick prick
sick slick stick thick tick trick wick

-ick rhymes with **-ic**

antiseptic attic basic comic elastic electric fantastic frantic
garlic lunatic magic music panic picnic plastic public
supersonic terrific tragic

Rr

rain rhyming sound **-ain**

again brain chain complain contain drain entertain explain
gain grain main obtain pain plain refrain remain Spain sprain
stain strain train vain

-ain rhymes with **-ane**

cane crane Jane lane mane
pane plane sane vane

Other words with different
spellings that rhyme with **rain**

reign rein vein

There was a young girl called Elaine
Who was dreadfully sick on the train –
Not once but **again** and **again**!

red   rhyming sound **-ed**

Ahmed bed bled bred fed fled Fred led
Mohammed moped red shed shred sled
sped Ted wed

-ed rhymes with some **-ead** words

ahead bread dead dread head
instead lead read spread thread
tread widespread

Another word with a
different spelling that
rhymes with **red**

said

There was a young boy called Ted
Who sped down the hill on a sled
One thing he'd forgotten
Was the shed at the bottom
And now Ted is nursing a sore head!

ride

rhyming sound **-ide**

aside   astride   beside   bride   collide   countryside   decide
divide   glide   guide   hide   inside   pride   provide   side
slide   stride   subdivide   tide   wide

-ide rhymes with some **-ied** words

cried   defied   denied   died   dried   fried   horrified   lied
replied   spied   terrified   tied   tried

Other words with different
spellings that rhyme with **ride**

dyed   eyed   I'd   sighed

deliver   liver   quiver   shiver   silver

It made me shake.
It made me shiver.
When the highwayman's ghost
Shouted,

"Stand
   and
     deliver!"

a b c d e f g h i j k l m n o p q **Rr** s t u v w x y z

road

rhyming sound **-oad**

goad   load   toad

-oad   rhymes with   **-ode**

code   episode   erode   explode   mode   ode   rode   strode

-oad   also rhymes with some   **-owed**   words

burrowed   crowed   flowed
glowed   mowed   owed
rowed   showed   slowed
snowed   stowed   towed

Here lies the body of a toad
Who forgot his Highway Code.
He didn't wait till the traffic slowed,
Before he tried to cross the road.

room

bedroom   bloom   boom   bridegroom   broom   doom   gloom   groom
heirloom   loom   mushroom   zoom

-oom   rhymes with   **-ume**

costume   flume   fume
perfume   plume

Other words with different
spellings that rhyme with **room**

tomb   whom   womb

A skeleton once in Khartoum
Invited a ghost to his room
They spent the whole night
In the eeriest fight
As to who should be frightened of whom.

rope — rhyming sound **-ope**

antelope   cope   dope   elope   envelope   grope
hope   horoscope   lope   microscope   mope   pope
scope   slope   telescope   tightrope

> Another word with a different
> spelling that rhymes with **rope**
>
> **soap**

**"I hope I can cope," said the antelope
As it started to walk along the tightrope.**

round — rhyming sound **-ound**

around   astound   background   bound
found   ground   hound   mound   pound
profound   sound   surround   wound

-ound rhymes with **-owned**

browned   clowned   crowned   downed
drowned   frowned   renowned

**My heart begins to pound
As I spin round and round,
On the whirling, twirling wheel
And I wish I was on the ground!**

rumble

rhyming sound **-umble**

bumble crumble fumble grumble humble jumble
mumble stumble tumble

rush

rhyming sound **-ush**

blush brush crush flush gush hush lush mush
plush shush slush thrush

Ss

score — rhyming sound -ore

adore ashore before bore carnivore chore core encore explore galore gore ignore more ore pore shore snore sore store swore therefore tore wore

-ore rhymes with -oar

boar oar roar soar

-ore also rhymes with -aw

caw claw craw draw flaw gnaw guffaw jackdaw jaw law outlaw paw raw saw seesaw straw thaw

> Other words with different spellings that rhyme with **score**
>
> corridor dinosaur door drawer floor for four indoor meteor nor or outdoor poor pour sure war your

shirt

rhyming sound **-irt**

dirt   flirt   skirt   squirt

-irt rhymes with **-urt**

blurt   curt   hurt   spurt

-irt also rhymes with **-ert**

advert   alert   Bert   concert   desert
dessert   expert   pert

shop

rhyming sound **-op**

bop   chop   clop   cop   crop   drop   flip-flop
flop   hop   lollipop   lop   mop   plop   pop
prop   shop   slop   stop   top

Another word with a
different spelling that
rhymes with **shop**

swap

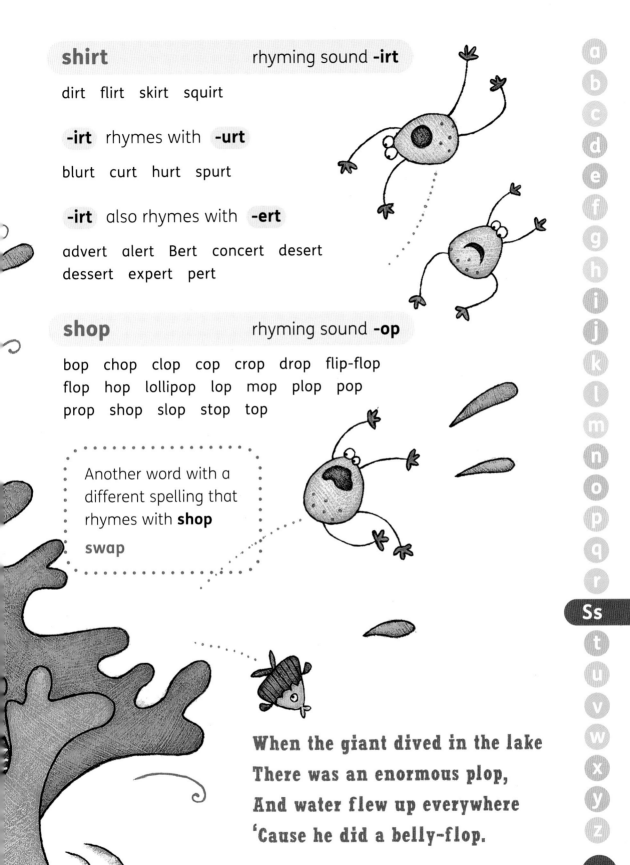

When the giant dived in the lake
There was an enormous plop,
And water flew up everywhere
'Cause he did a belly-flop.

smile

rhyming sound **-ile**

agile awhile crocodile file fragile hostile mile missile mobile pile profile reptile stile tile vile while

> Other words with different spellings that rhyme with **smile**
>
> aisle dial I'll isle style trial

Beware the smile of the crocodile
What he really wants to do
Is smile while he is chewing you!

snow

rhyming sound **-ow**

arrow below blow bow burrow crow elbow flow glow grow hedgerow know low marrow meadow mow pillow rainbow row scarecrow shadow shallow show slow sorrow sow stow throw tomorrow tow window

-ow rhymes with **-o**

ago armadillo buffalo Bruno commando Dae-ho disco domino echo go halo hello hero hippo logo macho mosquito no patio photo piano potato radio rodeo so solo stereo studio tornado UFO video volcano yo-yo zero

-ow also rhymes with **-oe**

doe foe hoe Joe mistletoe oboe toe woe

> Other words with different spellings that rhyme with **snow**
>
> although dough owe sew though

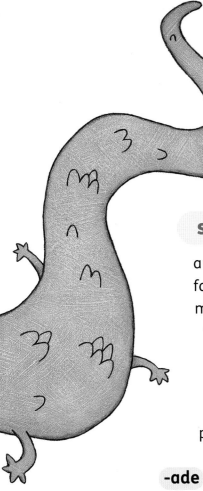

song   rhyming sound **-ong**

along belong bong ding-dong dong gong long oblong pong prong sarong strong throng tong wrong

spade   rhyming sound **-ade**

arcade barricade blade decade evade fade grade invade jade lemonade made marmalade parade persuade shade trade wade

-ade rhymes with **-aid**

afraid aid braid laid maid mermaid paid raid staid

-ade also rhymes with **-ayed**

arrayed betrayed decayed delayed frayed played prayed sprayed stayed strayed swayed X-rayed

Other words with different spellings that rhyme with **spade**

neighed obeyed preyed suede surveyed weighed

Jade shook
    the bottle
        of lemonade,
Then she opened it and we all got sprayed.

a b c d e f g h i j k l m n o p q r **Ss** t u v w x y z

speak

rhyming sound **-eak**

beak   bleak   creak   freak   leak   peak   sneak   squeak   streak   weak

-eak rhymes with **-eek**

cheek   creek   Greek   leek   meek   peek
reek   seek   sleek   week

Another word with a different spelling that rhymes with **speak**

shriek

-eak also rhymes with **-ique**

antique   boutique   clique   technique   unique

Two ghosts are playing hide-and-shriek.
They've been seeking each other since last week.

sport

rhyming sound **-ort**

airport export fort import passport port report
resort short snort sort support transport

-ort rhymes with **-aught**

caught distraught fraught onslaught taught

-ort also rhymes with **-ought**

bought brought fought nought ought sought thought

> Other words with different spellings that rhyme with **sport**
>
> astronaut court juggernaut quart taut thwart
> wart

stamp

rhyming sound **-amp**

amp camp champ clamp cramp damp
lamp ramp scamp tramp

storm
rhyming sound **-orm**

dorm   form   norm   perform   uniform

-orm   rhymes with some   **-arm**   words

swarm   warm

sun
rhyming sound **-un**

begun   bun   fun   gun   nun   pun   run   shun   spun   stun

-un   rhymes with some   **-one**   words

done   none   one   someone

-un   also rhymes with some   **-on**   words

son   ton   won

Other words with different spellings that rhyme with **sun**

certain   children   even garden   often   person question   woman written

Ss

swim

brim dim grim him Jim Kim prim rim
skim slim Tim trim whim

Other words with different
spellings that rhyme with **swim**

**gym   hymn   limb
pseudonym   synonym**

A rabbit raced a turtle.
The turtle easily won.
The rabbit came in second,
A little hot cross bun.

a b c d e f g h i j k l m n o p q r **Ss** t u v w x y z

Tt

A B C D E F G H I J K L M N O P Q R S Tt U V W X Y Z

table   rhyming sound **-able**

able cable fable stable timetable

tail   rhyming sound **-ail**

ail bail detail fail frail hail jail
mail nail pail quail rail sail snail
trail wail

> Another word with a different spelling that rhymes with **table**
>
> **label**

-ail rhymes with **-ale**

ale bale dale exhale female gale
impale inhale male nightingale pale
sale scale stale tale telltale whale

> Another word with a different spelling that rhymes with **tail**
>
> **veil**

talk   rhyming sound **-alk**

chalk   stalk   walk

-alk   rhymes with   **-ork**

cork   fork   pork   stork

-alk   also rhymes with   **-awk**

gawk   hawk   squawk   tomahawk

A whale in a veil getting married in a gale.

tent

accident   ascent   bent   cement   cent   compliment   consent   content
crescent   dent   descent   different   dissent   enjoyment   event
experiment   fragment   frequent   impatient   invent   irrelevant   lent
merriment   ornament   present   prevent   recent   relent   rent   resent
scent   sent   spent   torment   vent   went

-ent rhymes with some **-eant** words

leant   meant

-ent also rhymes with some **-ant** words

giant   important

We could not get rid of the scent
That a cow had left outside the tent!

tickle

rhyming sound **-ickle**

fickle   pickle   prickle   sickle   trickle

> Another word with a different spelling that rhymes with **tickle**
>
> **icicle**

Don't tickle a thistle or you'll get in a pickle,
For thistles are prickly and thistles'll prickle.

tie

rhyming sound **-ie**

die   lie   pie   untie

-ie rhymes with some **-y** words

ally   butterfly   by   cry   deny   dry   fly
fry   horrify   July   lay-by   lullaby   magnify
multiply   my   mystify   nearby   petrify   pigsty
pry   rely   reply   satisfy   shy   sky   sly   spy
sty   supply   terrify   try   why   wry

-ie also rhymes with **-igh**

high   sigh   thigh

> Other words with different spellings that rhyme with **tie**
>
> **alibi   buy   bye   dye   eye   goodbye guy   I**

time   rhyming sound -ime

chime   crime   grime   lime   mime   pantomime
prime   slime

> Other words with different spellings that rhyme with **time**
>
> **climb   enzyme   I'm   rhyme   thyme**

tower   rhyming sound -ower

cauliflower   cower   flower   glower   power   shower

-ower rhymes with some **-our** words

devour   flour   hour   our   scour   sour

town   rhyming sound -own

brown   clown   crown   down   drown   frown   gown

> Another word with a different spelling
> that rhymes with **town**
>
> **noun**

toy   rhyming sound -oy

ahoy   alloy   annoy   boy   buoy   convoy   corduroy
cowboy   coy   destroy   employ   enjoy   joy   ploy   Roy

tree
rhyming sound **-ee**

agree bee chimpanzee coffee degree disagree fee
flee free glee guarantee jamboree jubilee Lee knee
marquee pedigree referee refugee see settee spree
tee three toffee wee

-ee rhymes with **-ea**

flea pea plea sea tea

-ee rhymes with some **-y** words

any autobiography century city country every
everybody fancy February frisky intercity January
library many naughty ordinary party pretty quantity

> Other words with different spellings that rhyme with **tree**
>
> **be blackberry chimney donkey genie graffiti he
> history honey key macaroni me money monkey
> mystery pixie quay recipe she ski valley we**

trunk
rhyming sound **-unk**

bunk chipmunk chunk clunk drunk dunk hunk junk
punk shrunk skunk slunk stunk sunk

> Another word with a different spelling
> that rhymes with **trunk**
>
> **monk**

Tt

Uu

under   rhyming sound **-under**

blunder   plunder   thunder

> Another word with a
> different spelling that
> rhymes with **under**
>
> **wonder**

The pirates made a dreadful blunder
By trying to hide all their plunder
Beneath a tree during the thunder,
Now they're lying six feet under!

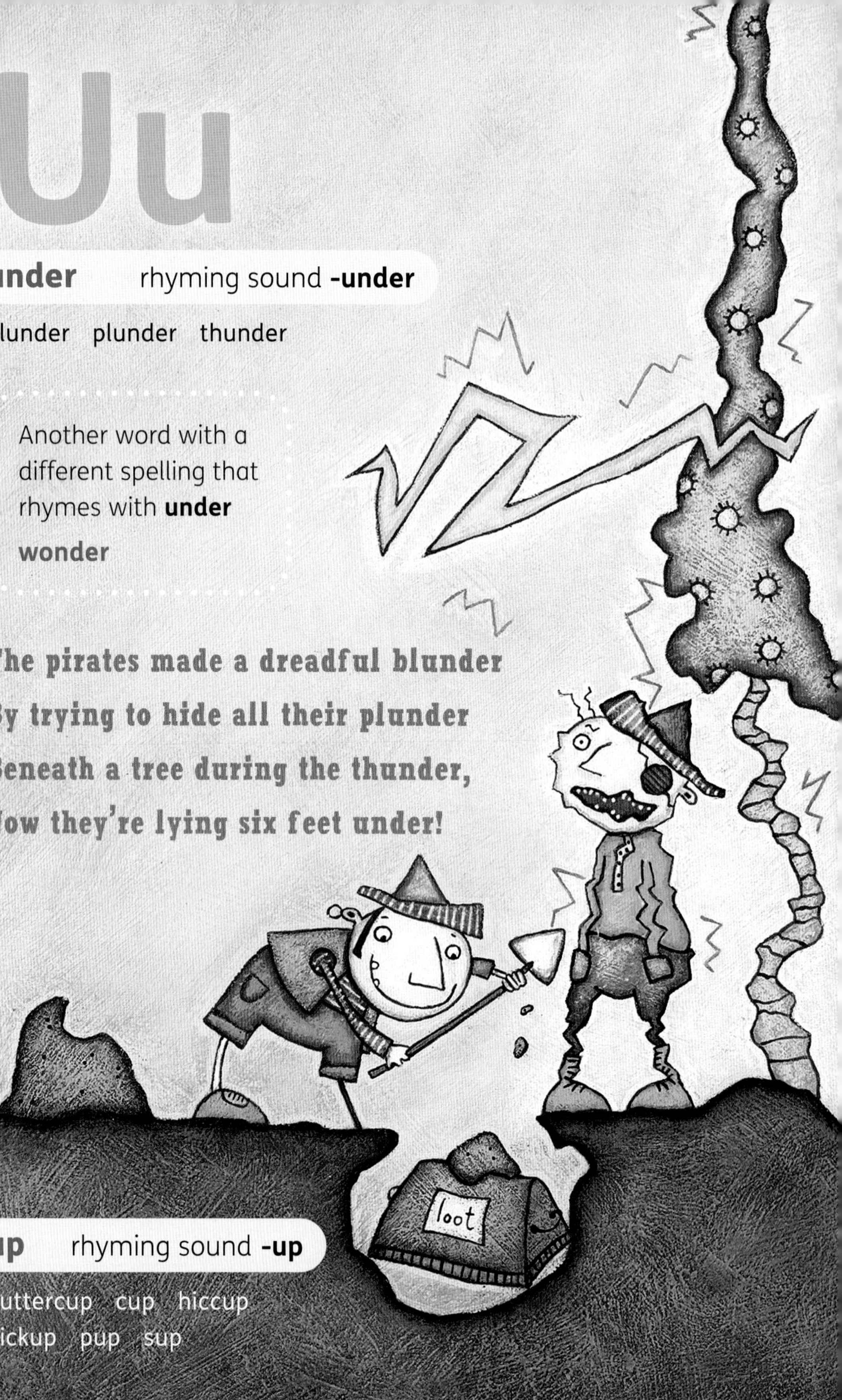

up   rhyming sound **-up**

buttercup   cup   hiccup
pickup   pup   sup

loot

urn

burn   churn   return   spurn   turn

-urn rhymes with **-earn**

earn   learn   yearn

-urn also rhymes with **-ern**

concern   fern   stern

us

bonus   bus   cactus   chorus   circus   crocus   genius   hippopotamus
minus   octopus   plus   pus   radius   thus   virus   walrus

-us rhymes with some **-uss** words

discuss   fuss

-us also rhymes with **-ous**

anxious   callous   courageous   courteous   curious   dangerous   dubious
enormous   envious   fabulous   famous   furious   glamorous   glorious
gorgeous   hideous   hilarious   horrendous   humorous   ingenious
jealous   ludicrous   marvellous   mischievous   monstrous   mountainous
mysterious   nervous   obvious   outrageous   precious   poisonous
raucous   ravenous   serious   spontaneous   tremendous   various
vigorous   wondrous

Other words with
different spellings
that rhyme with **-us**

Christmas
purpose

The driver caused an awful fuss
When we tried to board the bus
With our hippopotamus.

use

abuse   accuse   amuse   confuse   enthuse   excuse   fuse
muse   refuse   ruse

-use rhymes with **-ews**

chews   news   screws   stews

-use also rhymes with **-ues**

blues   clues   hues   queues

-use also rhymes with **-ooze**

ooze   snooze

Ewes who choose to read the news
Share their views in queues in zoos.

Other words with different spellings that rhyme with **-use**
**boos   choose   ewes   kangaroos   lose   tattoos
views   whose   zoos**

Vv

van

rhyming sound **-an**

an ban began bran can caravan catamaran clan deadpan fan flan gran Imran Japan man marzipan nan orang-utan pan plan ran scan span Stan superman tan than

Stan, Stan,
the lollipop man

Drives a blue and
yellow van

And washes his
socks in a frying
pan.

vest

rhyming sound **-est**

arrest bequest best chest conquest contest crest detest digest fattest freshest grandest guest happiest infest interest invest jest lest nest nicest pest protest quest quickest request rest saddest suggest test west zest

-est rhymes with **-essed**

addressed blessed caressed confessed depressed digressed distressed dressed expressed guessed impressed messed obsessed possessed pressed progressed stressed

Ww

wall rhyming sound **-all**

all ball call fall football hall
small squall stall tall

-all rhymes with **-awl**

bawl brawl crawl drawl
scrawl shawl sprawl trawl

-all also rhymes with **-aul**

caterwaul haul maul Paul

There was a young fellow called Paul
Who went to a fancy dress ball.
But he made a mistake
'Cause he went as a cake
And a dog ate him up in the hall.

weed

rhyming sound **-eed**

agreed bleed breed creed deed exceed
freed greed guaranteed heed indeed
need proceed reed refereed seed speed
steed succeed tweed

-eed rhymes with some **-ead** words

bead knead lead plead read

-eed also rhymes with some **-ede** words

centipede concede millipede stampede
swede

well

rhyming sound **-ell**

bell cell dwell farewell fell hell misspell
quell sell shell smell spell swell tell
unwell yell

Other words with different spellings that rhyme with **well**

caramel carousel excel gel hotel
lapel motel parallel propel rebel

Spinning round on the carousel
Sound the horn and ring the bell
Feel the fairground's magic spell
Spinning round on the carousel

wheel

rhyming sound **-eel**

eel feel heel keel kneel peel reel steel

-eel rhymes with **-eal**

appeal conceal deal heal ideal meal ordeal peal real reveal seal squeal steal veal zeal

win

rhyming sound **-in**

begin bin cabin chin coffin din dolphin fin goblin gremlin grin in javelin kin kitchen margin muffin origin penguin pin puffin pumpkin robin ruin satin sequin shin sin skin spin thin tin twin violin vitamin within

Other words with different spellings that rhyme with **win**

discipline examine imagine inn medicine women

When Violet plays her violin
She makes a really awful din.
I'm glad she hasn't got a twin!

Ww

wise

advertise advise anticlockwise arise clockwise disguise exercise
guise likewise prise revise rise sunrise surprise

-ise rhymes with some **-ies** words

cries dies dries flies fries horrifies lies lullabies petrifies pies
replies skies spies terrifies ties tries

-ise also rhymes with some **-ize** words

apologize capsize hypnotize idolize organize prize realize
recognize size

Other words with different spellings that rhyme with **wise**

buys eyes highs sighs thighs

worm

rhyming sound sounds like **-erm**

term

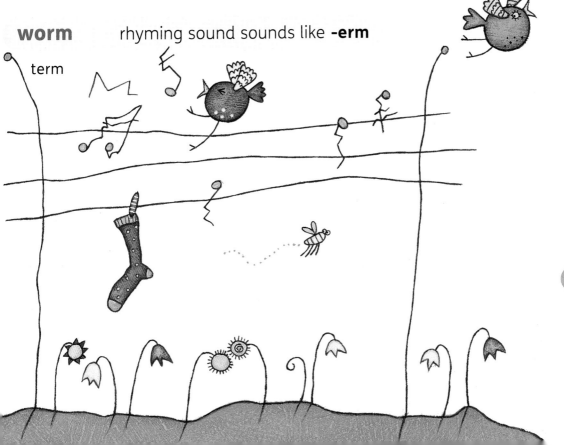

Xx

X-ray

rhyming sound **-ay**

alleyway anyway away bay betray birthday bray clay day
decay delay display essay fray hay holiday hooray hurray
lay may midday Monday (and all the other days of the week)
motorway okay pay pray railway ray say spray stay stowaway
straightaway subway sway takeaway today
tray way yesterday

-ay rhymes with **-eigh**

neigh sleigh weigh

-ay also rhymes with **-ey**

disobey grey hey obey prey
survey they

Other words with different
spellings that rhyme with **X-ray**

**ballet bouquet buffet
café chalet croquet
duvet fiancé(e) paté
ricochet sachet**

Xx

110

When Auntie Fay began to neigh
And spend the day just eating hay,
My uncle said, "I cannot say
Why she's behaving in this way.
I'd better put her in the stable
In the stall next to your
                    Auntie Mabel."

Yy

yard   rhyming sound **-ard**

bard   bombard   card   discard   farmyard
hard   lard   leotard   postcard   regard   shard

-ard rhymes with **-arred**

barred   charred   jarred   marred   scarred
sparred   starred   tarred

Another word with a different
spelling that rhymes with **yard**
guard

yellow rhyming sound **-ellow**

bellow fellow mellow

> Other words with
> different spellings that
> rhyme with **yellow**
>
> **cello   hello**

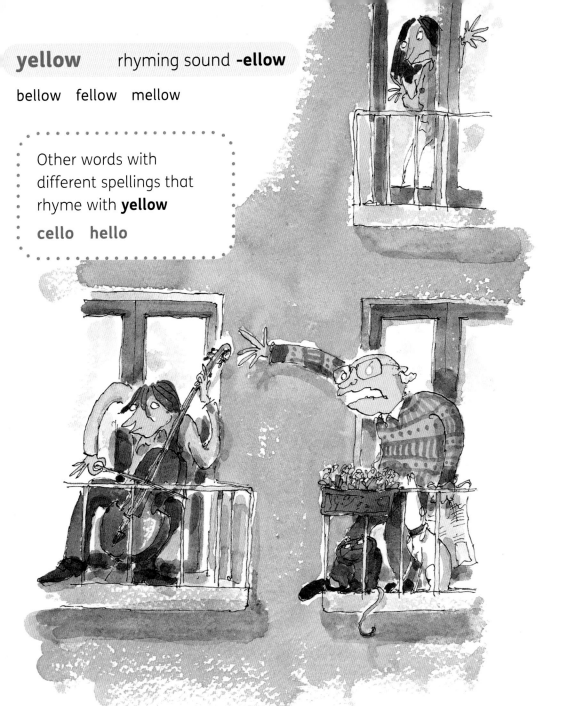

I was practising playing the cello,
When I heard someone give a loud bellow,
"For goodness sake
You make my ears ache.
Please stop it. There's a good fellow!"

Zz

zip
rhyming sound **-ip**

blip championship chip clip dip drip equip fingertip flip
friendship gossip grip hardship hip kip leadership lip microchip
nip paperclip pip quip rip ship sip skip slip snip strip tip
trip tulip whip

zoo
rhyming sound **-oo**

a-choo bamboo boo coo cuckoo hullaballoo igloo kangaroo loo
moo shampoo shoo tattoo too voodoo woo yoo-hoo

-oo rhymes with some **-ew** words

askew blew brew chew corkscrew crew
dew drew few flew grew interview knew
mew nephew new pew phew screw
shrew sinew skew slew threw view

-oo also rhymes with **-ue**

argue avenue barbecue blue clue
continue cue due flue fondue glue hue
queue rescue revue rue statue subdue
sue tissue true value venue

Other words with
different spellings
that rhyme with
zoo

**canoe do ewe
flu gnu guru
Hindu kung fu
menu Peru
redo rendezvous
shoe through
to tutu two
who you**

There was an old man from Peru
Who dreamed he was eating his shoe
He woke in the night
In a terrible fright
And found it was perfectly true.

Write your own poetry

Limericks

A limerick is a five-line verse which follows a set pattern. It was first made famous by the poet Edward Lear (1812-88). You can find examples of limericks on pages 48 (*There once was a boy called Bill*), and 115 (*There was an old man from Peru*).

In a limerick

- lines 1 and 2 are longer lines that end with a rhyme
- lines 3 and 4 are shorter lines that end with a rhyme
- line 5 is a longer line that rhymes with lines 1 and 2

Can you complete these limericks?

There was a young schoolboy
called Flynn
Who sat on a drawing pin
He leapt up in the air ...

You can find words with the rhyming sound **-in** listed under the entry for **win** on page 108, and words with the rhyming sound **-air** under the entry for **air** on page 8.

You can find words with the rhyming sound **-ee** listed under the entry for **tree** on page 99.

A daring young girl
from Dundee ...

A wizard's apprentice
called Matt ...

You can find words with the rhyming sound **-at** listed under the entry for **hat** on page 39.

Now see if you can make up a limerick on your own.
Try to think of a funny punchline to end it.

Nonsense nursery rhymes

Nonsense nursery rhymes are comical versions of traditional nursery rhymes. For example, here is the real nursery rhyme:

Mary had a little lamb,
Its fleece was white as snow
And everywhere that Mary went,
The lamb was sure to go.

And here is a nonsense version of it:

Mary had a little cow.
She fed it safety pins
And every time she milked the cow
The milk came out in tins.

Here are the first lines of some nonsense nursery rhymes. Can you complete them?

1 Sally had a little dog.
  She dressed it all in black...

2 Little Miss Petal
  Sat on a nettle...

3 Humpty Dumpty sat on the beach
  Watching the fish in the sea...

4 Millie, my sister, fell on her face
  She blamed it on me for not giving her space.

5 Little Bill Lofa sat on his sofa
  Eating the biggest iced cake...

6 Dr Bevan went to Devon...

7 Little Bo-Peep had a quick peek...

Counting rhymes

A counting rhyme is a rhyme which includes counting.
Some rhymes count up to ten, others count backwards from
10 down to 1.

Can you complete these counting rhymes?

One, Two
One, two
I'm off to the zoo
Three, four ... .

Ten Naughty Dragons
Ten naughty dragons blowing smoke-rings in a line,
One set himself on fire, then there were nine.

Nine naughty dragons ... .

Animal Counting Rhyme
One for the horse who's running off course.
Two for the cat in the big floppy hat,
Three for the ...

Ten Young Children
Ten young children
Playing in the park.
The first one said,
"Pretend I'm a shark."
The second one said,
"I'm a dinosaur."
The third one said ...

Rhyming riddles

The poems on this page are rhyming riddles.
Can you solve them?

1

I can spin. I can roll. I can fly through the air.
I go where you hit me. Then I lie waiting there.
I am usually round – sometimes big, sometimes small.
I can make my way over or back from a wall.
What am I?

2

My first is in ghoul and also in charm.
My second is in magic and twice in alarm.
My third is in cauldron but isn't in fire.
My fourth is in gremlin but not in vampire.

My fifth is in skeleton and in bones.
My sixth is in werewolf but isn't in groans.
My seventh is in spell but not in broomstick.
My eighth's found in treat, but not found
in trick.
My ninth is in phantom but isn't in fear.
My whole is the scariest night of the year.
What am I?

There is a rhyming riddle on page 46 too.

Answers: 1. ball 2. Halloween

3

Hold it steady in your hand,
Then you will see another land,
Where right is left, and left is right,
And no sound stirs by day or night;
When you look in, yourself you'll see,
Yet in that place you cannot be.

What am I?

Here is a riddle about an animal with the rhyming words missing.
Can you work out what the words are and what the animal is?

I scratch the leaves that have fallen ....
I am hard to see as my spines are ....
I use the strong claws upon my ....
To search for insects and slugs to ....
Soon I'll curl in a ball in my ....
And go to sleep for my winter ....

Make up a rhyming riddle of your own. Either choose a subject
yourself or write a riddle about an
animal or an object, such as
a pen, a book or a bicycle.

Answers: 3. mirror; down brown feet eat nest rest (hedgehog)

Rapping

Rapping is a type of rhyming poetry. A rap is a poem with plenty of rhyming and a very strong rhythm, which is often written to be performed to music.

Can you add some verses to this rap about people and their names?

Clap your hands, tap your feet,
Get the rhythm, get the beat.

My name's Grace. I am just ace.
I have got a smile on my face.

Clap your hands, tap your feet,
Get the rhythm, get the beat.

My name's Nasreen. I'm lean and mean.
I'm a star of the disco scene.

Clap your hands, tap your feet,
Get the rhythm, get the beat...

Can you write a fairground rap?
Here are two lines that you can use to get started:

C'mon everybody, let's go to the fair,
There's plenty of things for us to do there...

You can write a rap about any topic.

Choose your own subject and write a rap about it.
You could use these two lines to start your rap:

Come on everybody, let's hear you clap,
We're going to do the ... rap.

Rhyming couplets

One of the ways poets use rhymes is to write rhyming couplets.
A rhyming couplet is a pair of lines that rhyme. For example:

We like riding on the double-decker bus,
Up on the top-deck, that's the place for us!

Can you add some rhyming couplets to this list poem?

In My Magic Box
In my magic box, I will put

The twang of a guitar
The silver lining of a star

The juicy ripeness of a peach
The sunlight shining on a beach...

Chants

Many chants, like these traditional ones, are written in
rhyming couplets:

Teacher, Teacher
Teacher, teacher, please come quick
Tamsyn Brown's been terribly sick.

Can you complete these 'Teacher, teacher' chants?

Teacher, teacher, what should I do?...
Teacher, teacher, come and have a look...

I Know a Man...
I know a man who wears smelly socks.
I know a man who thinks he's a fox.

Can you complete these 'I know a man' chants?

I know a man with toes on his head ...
I know a man who lives in a drain ...

Homophones

A homophone is a word which sounds the same as another word, but it is spelled differently and has a different meaning.
For example, **hare** and **hair** are homophones.

Can you find the homophones in these rhymes?

Bare Bear hasn't any hair.
That's why Bare Bear is bare.

"No, I don't know what to do,"
I said to the man in the queue.
"So I'll take my cue from you."

A gnu who was new to the zoo
Asked another gnu what he should do.
The other gnu said,
Shaking his head,
"If I knew, I'd tell you, I'm new too!"

Now use this dictionary to find homophones for these words:

beach board great need pale pane pear read right road sell sew sore stair

Which of the above words has more than one other homophone?

Rhyme patterns

Many poems have four-line verses. A four-line verse is called a quatrain. Quatrains can have a number of different rhyming patterns.

Pattern 1

In this verse the first and second lines rhyme and the third and fourth lines rhyme.

As I was going out one day
My head fell off and rolled away.
But when I saw that it was gone,
I picked it up and put it on.

Can you complete the second verse of the poem?

And when I got into the ….
A fellow cried, "Look at your …!"
I looked at them and sadly …..
"I've left them both asleep in …!"

Pattern 2

This poem has verses in which the second line rhymes with the fourth line.

We are the gremlins.
We're up to no good.
We do things we shouldn't,
Not things that we should.

We get up to mischief
Of every sort.
But we're cunning and clever,
We never get caught.

Can you complete the next verse of the poem?

We are the gremlins.
We disconnect wires…

Can you add some more verses in the same pattern describing other things that the gremlins do?

Pattern 3

In this verse the first line rhymes with the third line and the second line rhymes with the fourth line.

When the night is as cold as stone,
When lightning severs the sky,
When your blood is chilled to the bone,
That's the hour when the witches fly.

Can you complete this verse about a mad magician using the same rhyme pattern?

In his dark cave the mad magician dwells...

Pattern 4

Sometimes poets write poems in which there is a rhyme within the line.

For example:

When Aunty Joan became a phone...

This is known as internal rhyme.

In the following verse the second line rhymes with the fourth line and there are internal rhymes in the first and third lines:

Elastic Jones had rubber bones.
He could bounce up and down like a ball.
When he was six, one of his tricks
Was jumping a ten-foot wall.

Can you complete this verse using the same rhyme pattern:

Ferdinand Fry boasted, "I can fly!"...

Now try to write a poem about a pirate called Peter the pirate in four-line verses, using one of these rhyming patterns.

Index of rhyming sounds

-eeze see *freeze*
-eg see *leg*
-eigh see *X-ray*
-el see *animal*
-el see *well*
-elf see *elf*
-ell see *well*
-ellow see *yellow*
-elt see *belt*
-en see *hen*
-end see *end*
-ene see *queen*
-ent see *tent*
-ept see *crept*
-er (as in her) see *fur*
-ere (as in here) see *ear*
-erm see *worm*

-ern see *urn*
-erry see *merry*
-ert see *shirt*
-ess see *dress*
-essed see *vest*
-est see *vest*
-et see *jet*
-etal see *nettle*
-ete see *meat*
-ette see *jet*
-ettle see *nettle*
-ever see *ever*
-ew (as in chew) see *zoo*
-ewed see *food*
-ews (as in news) see *use*
-ey (as in they) see *X-ray*

-ic see *quick*
-ice (as in ice) see *ice*
-ich see *itch*
-ick see *quick*
-ickle see *tickle*
-icks see *mix*
-id see *lid*
-iddle see *middle*
-ide see *ride*
-idge see *bridge*
-ie see *tie*
-ied see *ride*
-ies see *wise*
-ig see *big*
-igh see *tie*
-ight see *light*
-ign see *nine*
-ike see *bike*
-il see *ill*
-ile see *smile*
-ill see *ill*
-im see *swim*
-ime see *time*
-imp see *imp*
-in see *win*
-ind see *find*
-ine (as in magazine) see *queen*
-ine (as in fine) see *nine*
-ined see *find*
-ing see *king*
-ink see *ink*
-inner see *dinner*
-int see *print*
-ip see *zip*
-ique see *speak*
-ir see *fur*
-ird see *bird*
-ire see *fire*
-irl see *girl*
-irst see *first*
-irt see *shirt*
-ise (as in rise) see *wise*
-ish see *fish*

-iss see *kiss*
-issed see *mist*
-ist see *mist*
-it see *hit*
-itch see *itch*
-ite see *light*
-ive see *five*
-iver see *river*
-ix see *mix*
-ize see *wise*

-le see *animal*
-ly see *family*
-lly see *family*

-o (as in slow) see *snow*
-oad see *road*
-oak see *oak*
-oal see *hole*
-oar see *score*
-oard see *lord*
-oast see *post*
-oat see *coat*
-ob see *job*
-ock see *knock*
-ocks see *fox*
-ode see *road*
-oe see *snow*
-oes see *nose*
-og see *dog*
-ogue see *dog*
-oil see *oil*
-oke see *oak*
-old see *old*
-ole see *hole*
-oll see *hole*
-on (as in son) see *sun*
-ond see *pond*
-one (as in phone) see *bone*
-one (as in one) see *sun*
-oney see *honey*
-ong see *song*
-oo see *zoo*

-ood (as in food) see *food*

-ood (as in wood) see *hood*

-ooed see *food*

-ook see *cook*

-ool see *pool*

-oom see *room*

-oon see *moon*

-oop see *hoop*

-oot see *boot*

-ooze see *use*

-op see *shop*

-ope see *rope*

-or see *score*

-ord see *lord*

-ore see *score*

-ored see *lord*

-ork see *talk*

-orm see *storm*

-orn see *corn*

-ort see *sport*

-os (as in radios) see *nose*

-ose see *nose*

-oss see *boss*

-ost see *post*

-ot see *pot*

-ote see *coat*

-other see *brother*

-ouble see *bubble*

-ough (as in rough) see *puff*

-ough (as in plough) see *cow*

-ought see *sport*

-ould see *hood*

-ounce see *bounce*

-ound see *round*

-oup see *hoop*

-our (as in hour) see *tower*

-ous see *us*

-ouse see *house*

-out see *out*

-ove see *love*

-ow (as in now) see *cow*

-ow (as in blow) see *snow*

-owed see *road*

-owel see *owl*

-ower see *tower*

-owl see *owl*

-own see *town*

-own (as in phone, groan) see *bone*

-owned (as in crowned) see *round*

-ows see *nose*

-ox see *fox*

-oy see *toy*

-oyal see *oil*

-shu see *brochure*

-sion see *musician*

-ssion see *musician*

-tion see *musician*

-ub see *grub*

-ubble see *bubble*

-uck see *duck*

-ud see *mud*

-ude see *food*

-ue see *zoo*

-ued see *food*

-ues (as in clues) see *use*

-uff see *puff*

-ug see *jug*

-ul see *animal*

-ul see *pull*

-ule see *pool*

-ull see *pull*

-um see *mum*

-umb see *mum*

-umble see *rumble*

-ume see *room*

-ump see *jump*

-un see *sun*

-unch see *lunch*

-under see *under*

-une see *moon*

-ung see *lung*

-unk see *trunk*

-unny see *honey*

-unt see *hunt*

-up see *up*

-ur see *fur*

-url see *girl*

-urn see *urn*

-urt see *shirt*

-us see *us*

-use see *use*

-ush see *rush*

-uss see *us*

-ust see *dust*

-ut see *hut*

-ute see *boot*

-y see *tie*

-y see *tree*

A to Z index

cape 36
capital 9
capsize 109
capsule 74
car 16
caramel 106
caravan 103
card 112
cardboard 57
care 8
career 26
careful 76
caressed 103
carnivore 86
carousel 106
carpet 50
carries 33
cart 17
cartoon 61
case 28
cash 21
cashier 26
cask 9
Caspar 34
casserole 40
cassette 50
cast 54
cat 39
catalogue 24
catamaran 103
catch 17
caterwaul 105
caught 91
cauliflower 98
cavalier 26
cave 17
caviar 16
caw 86
ceased 27
ceiling 52
celebrate 35
cell 106
cello 113

cement 96
cent 96
centipede 106
centre 34
century 99
certain 92
chain 78
chair 8
chalet 110
chalk 95
champ 91
championship 114
chance 22
chap 58
character 34
charm 9
charred 112
chart 17
chase 28
chased 73
chat 39
cheap 52
cheat 59
check 66
cheek 90
cheep 52
cheer 26
cheerful 76
cheese 33
chemist 60
cheque 66
cherry 60
chess 25
chest 103
chestnut 45
chew 114
chewed 31
chews 102
chick 77
chicks 60
chief 18
childhood 44

children 92
chill 48
chime 98
chimney 99
chimneys 33
chimp 49
chimpanzee 99
chimpanzees 33
chin 108
chink 49
chip 114
chipmunk 99
choir 29
choke 69
choose 102
chop 87
chord 57
chore 86
chorus 101
chose 68
Christmas 101
chuck 25
chug 51
chum 62
chunk 99
churn 101
chute 13
cigar 16
circle 9
circuit 39
circus 101
city 99
clad 22
claim 64
clamp 91
clan 103
clang 10
clank 10
clap 58
clarinet 50
clash 21
class 36
classed 54

claw 86
clay 110
clean 77
clear 26
clever 27
click 77
clicks 60
climb 98
cling 52
clink 49
clip 114
clique 90
cloak 69
clock 53
clocks 32
clockwise 109
clog 24
clone 12
clop 87
close 68
clot 75
clout 71
clown 98
clowned 84
club 37
cluck 25
clue 114
clues 102
clump 51
clung 57
clunk 99
coal 40
coast 74
coat 18
cob 51
code 82
coffee 99
coffin 108
cog 24
coil 69
coke 69
cold 70
collide 80

collision 63
combat 39
combine 67
come 62
comic 77
comically 29
commando 88
commonplace 28
compact 8
compare 8
compete 59
complain 78
complete 59
completely 29
completion 63
compliment 96
comprehension 63
conceal 108
concede 106
concentrate 35
concert 87
concrete 59
cone 12
confess 25
confession 63
confessed 103
confiscate 35
confuse 102
confusion 63
conquest 103
consent 96
consider 34
console 40
consoled 70
contact 8
contain 78
content 96
contest 103
continue 114
contract 8
contrary 38

contrast 54
controlled 70
convoy 98
coo 114
cooed 31
cook 18
cool 74
coop 44
cop 87
cope 84
copier 34
copies 33
copying 52
cord 56
corduroy 98
core 86
cork 95
corkscrew 114
corn 19
corridor 86
costume 83
cot 75
could 44
country 99
countryside 80
courageous 101
courgette 50
court 91
courteous 101
cow 20
cowboy 98
cower 98
cox 32
coy 98
crab 20
crack 12
cracked 8
crag 30
cram 50
cramp 91
crane 78
crank 10

dubious 101
duck 25
dud 62
due 114
duet 50
duff 76
dug 51
dugout 71
dumb 62
dump 51
dune 61
dung 57
dungarees 33
dunk 99
dust 25
duvet 110
dwell 106
dwelt 11
dye 97
dyed 80
dynamite 56

E
each 10
ear 26
earl 36
early 29
earn 101
earshot 75
earwig 11
ease 33
east 27
eat 59
echo 88
educate 35
eel 108
effect 8
egg 55
eight 35
elastic 77
elbow 88
elbows 68
electric 77

electrician 63
elegant 9
elephant 9
elf 27
elope 84
embark 23
embrace 28
embraced 73
empire 29
employ 98
encore 86
end 27
engage 72
engineer 26
enjoy 98
enjoyment 96
enormous 101
enough 76
enrage 72
entertain 78
enthuse 102
entrance 22
envelope 84
envious 101
enzyme 98
episode 82
equip 114
erode 82
escape 36
essay 110
estate 35
estimate 35
evade 89
even 92
event 96
ever 27
every 99
everybody 99
ewe 114
ewes 102
exact 8
exaggerate 35
exam 50

examine 108
exceed 106
excel 106
except 21
excess 25
excite 56
exclaim 64
exclude 31
excuse 102
execute 13
exercise 109
exhale 94
exit 39
expand 38
expansion 63
experiment 96
expert 87
explain 78
explode 82
explore 86
explored 57
export 91
expose 68
express 25
expressed 103
expression 63
extend 27
extension 63
extract 8
extreme 24
eye 97
eyebrow 20
eyed 80
eyes 109

F
fab 20
fable 94
fabulous 101
face 28
faced 73
fact 8
fad 22

fade 89
fail 94
faint 73
fair 8
fairy 38
faithful 76
fake 54
fall 105
falsehood 44
fame 64
family 29
famous 101
fan 103
fancy 99
fang 10
fanned 38
fantastic 77
far 16
fare 8
farewell 106
farm 9
farmyard 112
fascinate 35
fast 54
fat 39
fate 35
father 34
fatter 34
fattest 103
favourite 39
fawn 19
fear 26
fearful 76
feast 27
feat 59
February 99
fed 79
fee 99
feel 108
fees 33
feet 59
fell 106
fellow 113

felt 11
female 94
fen 39
fern 101
ferry 60
fete 35
fettle 66
few 114
fiancé(e) 110
fickle 97
fiction 63
fiddle 60
fidget 50
fig 11
fight 56
file 88
fill 48
fin 108
finally 29
find 29
fine 67
fined 29
fingertip 114
fir 34
fire 29
fireplace 28
first 29
fish 30
fist 60
fit 39
five 30
fix 60
flab 20
flag 30
flair 8
flake 54
flame 64
flan 103
flap 58
flapjack 12
flash 21
flask 9
flat 39

flaw 86
flea 99
fleas 33
fleck 66
fled 79
flee 99
flees 33
fleet 59
flew 114
flick 77
flicks 60
flies 109
flight 56
fling 52
flint 75
flip 114
flip-flop 87
flirt 87
flit 39
float 18
flock 53
flocks 32
flog 24
flood 62
floor 86
flop 87
floss 14
flounce 14
flour 98
flow 88
flowed 82
flower 98
flown 12
flows 68
flu 114
flue 114
fluff 76
flume 83
flung 57
flush 85
flute 13
fly 97
flyer 29

jubilee 99
jug 51
juggernaut 91
July 97
jumble 85
jump 51
jumper 34
jumping 52
June 61
junk 99
just 25
jut 45

K

kangaroo 114
kangaroos 102
Kate 35
kayak 12
kebab 20
keel 108
keen 77
keep 52
keg 55
Ken 39
kept 21
kettle 66
key 99
keyboard 57
keys 33
kick 77
kicks 60
kid 55
kidnap 58
kill 48
Kim 93
kin 108
kind 29
kindness 25
king 52
kink 49
kip 114
kiss 53
kissed 60

kit 39
kitchen 108
kite 56
knack 12
knave 17
knead 106
knee 99
kneel 108
knees 33
knelt 11
knew 114
knight 56
knit 39
knob 51
knock 53
knockout 71
knocks 32
knot 75
know 88
known 12
knows 68
kung fu 114

L

lab 20
label 94
lace 28
laced 73
lack 12
lacked 8
lad 22
ladybird 11
lagoon 61
laid 89
lair 8
lake 54
lamb 50
lame 64
lamp 91
lance 22
land 38
landmark 23
landscape 36

lane 78
lank 10
lap 58
lapel 106
lard 112
lark 23
lash 21
last 54
latch 17
late 35
launderette 50
law 86
lawn 19
lay 110
lay-by 97
lead 79
lead 106
leadership 114
leak 90
lean 77
leant 96
leap 52
leapt 21
learn 101
least 27
led 79
leek 90
leer 26
leg 55
lemonade 89
Len 39
lend 27
lent 96
leotard 112
leprechaun 19
less 25
lest 103
let 50
liar 29
library 99
lice 46
lick 77
licks 60

lid 55
lie 97
lied 80
lies 109
light 56
like 11
likewise 109
limb 93
lime 98
limerick 77
limitation 63
limiting 52
limousine 77
limp 49
line 67
lined 29
link 49
lint 75
lip 114
liquid 55
liquorice 30
list 60
lit 39
little 9
live 30
liver 81
load 82
loan 12
lob 51
lock 53
locks 32
log 24
logo 88
lollipop 89
lone 12
loneliness 25
long 89
loo 114
look 18
lookout 71
loom 83
loop 44
loot 13

lop 87
lope 84
lord 57
lose 102
loss 14
lot 75
louse 44
lout 71
love 57
low 88
loyal 69
luck 25
ludicrous 101
lug 51
lullabies 109
lullaby 97
lumberjack 12
lump 51
lunatic 77
lunch 57
lung 57
lush 85

M

ma 16
mac 12
macaroni 99
macaroon 61
machine 77
macho 88
mad 22
made 89
magazine 77
magician 63
magnet 50
magnify 97
maid 89
mail 94
maim 64
main 78
make 54
male 94
man 103

mane 78
maniac 12
manned 38
many 99
map 58
mare 8
margin 108
marigold 70
mark 23
marmalade 89
maroon 61
marquee 99
marred 112
marrow 88
marvellous 101
Mary 38
marzipan 103
mascot 75
mash 21
mask 9
mast 54
mat 39
match 17
matchsticks 60
mate 35
mathematician 63
matrix 60
maul 105
may 110
me 99
meadow 88
meadows 68
meal 108
mean 77
meant 96
meat 59
medal 9
meddle 9
medicine 108
meek 90
meet 59
Meg 55

satin 108	screen 77	settle 66	shooed 31	sill 48	sleigh 110
satisfy 97	screw 114	sever 27	shook 18	simply 29	slept 21
save 17	screwed 31	severe 26	shoot 13	sin 108	slew 114
saw 86	screws 102	sew 88	shootout 71	sincere 26	slewed 31
sawn 19	scrimp 49	sewn 12	**shop 87**	sinew 114	slice 46
say 110	scroll 40	sews 68	shore 86	sing 52	slick 77
scab 20	scrub 37	shack 12	shorn 19	sink 49	slid 55
scaffold 70	scruff 76	shade 89	short 91	sinner 24	slide 80
scale 94	scrum 62	shadow 88	shot 75	sip 114	slight 56
scam 50	scrunch 57	shadows 68	should 44	sir 34	slim 93
scamp 91	scud 62	shake 54	shout 71	sister 34	slime 98
scan 103	scuff 76	shallow 88	shove 57	sit 39	sling 52
scanned 38	scum 62	sham 50	show 88	site 56	slink 49
scant 9	sea 99	shame 64	showed 82	six 60	slip 114
scar 16	seal 108	shampoo 114	shower 98	size 109	slipper 34
scare 8	seam 24	shampooed 31	shown 12	skate 35	sliver 81
scarecrow 88	seas 33	shape 36	shows 68	skateboard 57	slog 24
scarred 112	seat 59	shard 112	shrank 10	skew 114	sloop 44
scary 38	secret 50	share 8	shred 79	ski 99	slop 87
scene 77	section 63	shark 23	shrew 114	skid 55	slope 84
scent 96	see 99	shave 17	shriek 90	skies 109	slot 75
schedule 74	seed 106	shawl 105	shrill 48	skill 48	slow 88
scheme 24	seek 90	she 99	shrimp 49	skim 93	slowed 82
school 74	seem 24	shear 26	shrine 67	skimp 49	slows 68
scold 70	seen 77	shed 79	shrink 49	skin 108	slug 51
scoop 44	seep 52	sheen 77	shrub 37	skint 75	slum 62
scoot 13	sees 33	sheep 57	shrug 51	skip 114	slump 51
scope 84	seesaw 86	sheer 26	shrunk 99	skirt 87	slung 57
score 86	seize 33	sheet 59	shun 92	skis 33	slunk 99
scoreboard 57	self 27	shelf 27	shunt 45	skunk 99	slur 34
scored 57	selfish 30	shell 106	shush 85	sky 97	slush 85
scorn 19	sell 106	shin 108	shut 45	slab 20	sly 97
Scot 75	send 27	shine 67	shy 97	slack 12	smack 12
scour 98	sensation 63	ship 114	sick 77	slam 50	smacked 8
scout 71	sent 96	**shirt 87**	sickle 97	slang 10	small 105
scowl 71	separate 35	shiver 81	side 80	slap 58	smart 17
scram 50	sequin 108	shoal 40	sigh 97	slapdash 21	smash 21
scrap 58	serene 77	shock 53	sighed 80	slash 21	smear 26
scrape 36	serious 101	shocks 32	sighs 109	slate 35	smell 106
scratch 17	service 53	shockwave 17	sight 56	sled 79	**smile 88**
scrawl 105	serviette 50	shoe 114	sign 67	sleek 90	smoke 69
scream 24	set 50	shoelace 28	signed 29	sleep 52	smother 14
screech 10	settee 99	shoo 114	signpost 74	sleet 59	smug 51

snack 12
snacked 8
snag 30
snail 94
snake 54
snap 58
snare 8
snatch 17
sneak 90
sneer 26
sneeze 33
snip 114
snitch 49
snob 51
snoop 44
snooze 102
snore 86
snored 57
snort 91
snot 75
snout 71
snow 88
snowed 82
snowflake 54
snows 68
snub 37
snuff 76
snug 51
so 88
soak 69
soap 84
soar 86
soared 57
sob 51
sock 53
socks 32
software 8
soil 69
sold 70
sole 40
soled 70
solitaire 8
solitude 31

solo 88
some 62
someone 92
son 92
song 89
soon 61
sore 86
sorrow 88
sort 91
sought 91
sound 84
soundtrack 12
soup 44
sour 98
souvenir 26
sow 20
sow 88
sown 12
sows 68
space 28
spaced 73
spade 89
Spain 78
spanned 38
spar 16
spare 8
spark 23
sparred 112
spat 39
speak 90
spear 26
special 9
speck 66
sped 79
speech 10
speed 106
spell 106
spelt 11
spend 27
spent 96
sphere 26
spice 46
spied 80

spies 109
spike 11
spill 48
spin 108
spine 67
spinner 24
spire 29
spite 56
splash 21
splat 39
spleen 77
splice 46
splint 75
split 39
spoil 69
spoke 69
spool 74
spoon 61
spontaneous 101
sport 91
spot 75
spouse 44
spout 71
sprain 78
sprang 10
sprawl 105
spray 110
sprayed 89
spread 79
spree 99
sprig 11
spring 52
sprint 75
sprite 56
sprung 57
spud 62
spun 92
spur 34
spurn 101
spurt 87
spy 97
squall 105

square 8
squat 75
squawk 95
squeak 90
squeal 108
squeeze 33
squid 55
squint 75
squire 29
squirrel 9
squirt 87
squish 30
stab 20
stable 94
stack 12
stacked 8
stag 30
stage 72
stagefright 56
staid 89
stain 78
stair 8
staircase 28
stake 54
stale 94
stalk 95
stall 105
stamp 91
stampede 106
Stan 103
stance 22
stand 38
stank 10
star 16
stare 8
starred 112
start 17
state 35
station 63
statue 114
stay 110
stayed 89
steak 54

steal 108
steam 24
steed 106
steel 108
steep 52
steer 26
stepped 21
stereo 88
stereos 68
stern 101
stews 102
stick 77
sticks 60
stile 88
still 48
sting 52
stink 49
stir 34
stirred 11
stitch 49
stoat 18
stock 53
stocks 32
stole 40
stone 12
stood 44
stool 74
stoop 44
stop 87
store 86
stored 57
stork 95
storm 92
stout 71
stow 88
stowaway 110
stowed 82
stows 68
straight 35
straightaway 110
strain 78
strand 38

strap 58
straw 86
strayed 89
streak 90
stream 24
street 59
stress 25
stressed 103
strewn 61
stride 80
strike 11
string 52
strip 114
strive 30
strode 82
stroke 69
stroll 40
strolled 70
strong 89
struck 25
strum 62
strung 57
strut 45
stub 37
stubble 15
stuck 25
stud 62
studio 88
stuff 76
stumble 85
stump 51
stun 92
stung 57
stunk 99
stunt 45
stupid 55
sty 97
style 88
subdivide 80
subdue 114
subheading 52
submarine 77
substitute 13

tram 50
tramp 91
trampoline 77
trance 22
tranquil 48
transport 91
trap 58
trapeze 33
trash 21
trawl 105
travel 9
tray 110
tread 79
treat 59
tree 99
trees 33
trek 66
tremendous 101
trend 27
trespass 36
trial 88
trick 77
trickle 97
tricks 60
tried 80
tries 109
trike 11
trim 93
trip 114
troll 40
trombone 12
troop 44
trot 75
trouble 15
trounce 14
trout 71
trowel 71
truck 25
true 114
trump 51
trumpet 50
trunk 99
trust 25

try 97
tsar 16
tub 37
tuck 25
tug 51
tulip 114
tum 62
tumble 85
tune 61
tunnel 9
turmoil 69
turn 101
tut-tut 45
tutu 114
twang 10
tweed 106
twice 46
twiddle 60
twig 11
twilight 56
twin 108
twine 67
twirl 36
twist 60
twit 37
twitch 49
two 114
tycoon 61
typhoon 61
tyre 29

U
UFO 88
UFOs 68
umpire 29
under 100
understand 38
understood 44
undid 55
unfair 8
unfurl 36
unicorn 19
uniform 92

unique 90
unite 56
unkind 29
unless 25
unpack 12
unpacked 8
untie 97
until 48
unwell 106
unwrap 58
up 100
upright 56
upset 50
upstage 72
uptight 56
urn 101
us 101
use 102
useful 76
usual 9
usually 29
utmost 74

V
vain 78
valentine 67
valley 99
value 114
vampire 29
van 103
vane 78
vanish 30
various 101
vary 38
vast 54
vat 39
veal 108
veer 26
veil 94
vein 78
vent 96
venue 114
very 60

vest 103
vet 50
vice 46
video 88
videos 68
view 114
viewed 31
views 102
vigorous 101
vile 88
village 103
vine 67
violin 108
virus 101
visit 39
vitamin 108
volcano 88
volcanoes 68
vole 40
volunteer 26
voodoo 114
vote 18
vow 20
vowel 71

W
wade 89
wag 30
wage 72
wail 94
waist 73
wait 35
wake 54
walk 95
wall 105
walrus 101
wand 73
wander 34
war 86
ward 57
warm 92
wart 91
wary 38

waste 73
water 34
wave 17
way 110
we 99
weak 90
wean 77
wear 8
weather 34
website 56
wed 79
wee 99
weed 106
week 90
weep 52
weigh 110
weighed 89
weight 35
weir 26
well 106
welt 11
went 96
wept 21
were 34
west 103
wet 50
whack 12
whacked 8
whale 94
wham 50
what 75
whatever 27
wheat 59
wheel 108
wheeze 33
when 39
whenever 27
where 8
wherever 27
which 49
whichever 27
while 88
whim 93

whine 67
whined 29
whip 114
whiplash 21
whirl 36
whirligig 11
whirlpool 74
whirr 34
whirred 11
white 56
who 114
whoever 27
whole 40
whom 83
whoop 44
whose 102
why 97
wick 77
wide 80
widespread 79
wig 11
wigwam 50
will 48
wimp 49
win 108
wind 29
windmill 48
window 88
wine 67
wing 52
wink 49
winner 24
winter 34
wire 29
wise 109
wish 30
wit 39
witch 49
within 108
without 71
woe 88
woes 68
woke 69

143